THE MEXICAN AMERICAN IN THE SCHOOLS: PROTOTYPE FOR IN-SERVICE PROGRAMS ON THE MEXICAN AMERICAN

By: LUIS F. HERNANDEZ-PRADEAU

San Francisco, California
1977

Published by

R & E RESEARCH ASSOCIATES, INC.
4843 Mission Street
San Francisco, California 94112

Publishers
Robert D. Reed and Adam S. Eterovich

Library of Congress Card Catalog Number
76-27001

I.S.B.N.
0-88247-421-9

TABLE OF CONTENTS

LIST OF TABLES

CHAPTER I

INTRODUCTION

In January, 1972 at the Hispanic Urban Center in Los Angeles, 158 principals, coordinators, and teachers from East Los Angeles elementary schools participated in an in-service program titled The Mexican American in the Schools. The objective of the project was to raise the expectation of the elementary school professionals as it related to the Mexican American child by acquiring cognitive knowledge of the culture, history, and current problems of the Mexican American community.[1]

The inception of The Mexican American in the Schools in-service program had taken place during the early summer of 1971, when the Reverend Vahac Mardirosian, Director of the Hispanic Urban Center and for several years a leader for better education in the Chicano Movement, requested the development of an in-service program. The goal of the program would be to alter teacher expectation in terms of Mexican American youngsters so as to eventuate in improved reading achievement and amelioration of drop-out rate of these students.

Reverend Mardirosian based his request for such a program on data published by the Los Angeles Unified School District which clearly showed that children in schools with large minority enrollment (over 75%) were far behind their Anglo peers in reading achievement.[2] After studying the various programs offered by the Los Angeles Unified School District to alleviate persistent low achievement levels, the Reverend Mardirosian attributed the continued lack of academic achievement by a high percentage of Mexican American youngsters to their low reading level and established a causal relationship with the drop-out rate among these students. He also concluded that lack of achievement would continue as long as the Anglo teachers of the Mexican American students remained unaware of the conflicts created by cultural differences between the teachers and Mexican American students.

Both Mardirosian and the developer[3] of the program were well aware of the various other reasons advanced by pedagogical thesis for the low achievement scores and the high drop-out rate common to Chicano students. Among those given as predominant causes were: ineffective instructional systems, children's lack of proficiency in English, negative or neutral home influences. But educational research in the area of self-fulfilling prophecy, documented by Robert Rosenthal and Lenore Jacobson in Pygmalion in the Classroom, and the work of Manuel Ramirez at University California at Riverside relative to the learning style of children of various cultural backgrounds, led to the hypothesis that the teacher unwittingly contributed to achievement deficit through his low expectation of minority children. A concomitant cause was believed to be the teacher's teaching pattern which conflicted with the home training of the Mexican American child.

Proceeding on this empirical evidence, the director of the Hispanic Urban Center worked through a community advisory committee to develop educational strategy for disseminating information and developing awareness. This paper will attempt to describe the formation, development, and implementation of that strategy and to relate its repercussions on state legislation mandating creation of staff-development programs that address themselves to this issue.

1

Statement of Purpose

The purpose of this paper is to substantiate that the in-service program, The Mexican American in the Schools, achieved its objective--that of modifying elementary school teachers' and administrators' cognitive knowledge of the cultural differences among the Mexican American students. The study will show that the community originated the program, established the guidelines and submitted the program for acceptance to the accrediting agent, the funding agents, and the Los Angeles Unified Schools for approval for teacher participation in the program. In addition, the paper will assert that the Hispanic Urban Center program anticipated the content of the areas of emphasis determined by the guidelines of Article 3.3, Sections 13345 - 13345 - 13349 of the State of California, Education Code; and that the program subsequently served as a model for in-service programs designed to implement effective relationships between school staffs and the minority pupils of Mexican American descent in attendance at public schools.

Significance of the Study

The Mexican American in the Schools is the outcome of pressure created by a group of citizens from an East Los Angeles community made up mainly from members of the Chicano Coalition. Their action was motivated by discontent with efforts of the school district to raise the low achievement scores of the Mexican American students in various schools. The continued reports of depressed achievement scores[4] published by the Los Angeles Unified Schools indicated to the community the district's persistent failure and unproductive attempts to create change for the Mexican American youngster. Once this cause-effect relationship was comprehended by the community, it activated the decision to offer an alternative educational strategy that could possibly affect the desired change. This resolve led to the creation of the Hispanic Urban Center and the program housed there. This overt action may be interpreted as a response to the general request by schools for parental involvement and a correction to the somewhat popular premise that Mexican American parents do not care about the education of their children.

The Mexican American in the Schools was a program developed specifically for the Los Angeles Unified Schools; however, the program was available to any school district that wanted to participate. One of the unique features of the program was the cadre of experts that were responsible for the leadership and implementation of the program. The qualifications for leadership, generally as an instructor, required community approval. The requisites for the position were specific. The candidate was expected not only to have met city and state credential requirements, but also to have teaching experience in the schools of the barrio.[5] The candidate needed to be familiar with the variations and differences among the various groups within the barrio. Additionally, it was expected that the potential leader would have knowledge of the language interferences and an understanding of the barrio dialects. Equally specified was commitment to the Chicano Movement, the latter demonstrable only in terms of popularly known involvement by the candidate in the activities for change originating within the barrio.

The program was perceived as an experiment not only in presenting community know-how in dealing with an issue that the school district had failed to remove, but also as a base from which to develop teaching strategies for those areas of weakness in the education of the Mexican American youngster in the schools. The criticism was not to disparage but, rather, to show why the action censured had failed to meet success with Mexican American students. The operative premise was that comparison of differences would affect change.

Once the expected awareness was established, the school staff member could then be presented the empirical evidence that might lead to the development of methods and techniques that would lead to the improvement of learning for the Mexican American child.

Of note is the evaluative tool the program produced. The potential value of this instrument may lie not so much in measuring growth of cognitive learning on the part of the participants in the program, but rather, in its screening for teachers who might be better suited for teaching in areas with a paucity of Mexican American students.

Research Questions

The questions to which this paper is addressed are:

1. How did the community determine the need for a community initiated in-service program on the Mexican American in the schools?

2. What was the content of the program, The Mexican American in the Schools?

3. What did the evaluations determine about the program?

4. What were the "spin-offs" resulting from this effort?

Definition of Terms

The following terms are given these operative meanings in the course of this paper. (Some of these terms lack authoritative definition, for as yet, no definitive work includes their formal denotation.)

Chicano. A Mexican American who identifies with the Chicano Movement.

Chicano Movement. An action group within the Mexican American community committed to bringing about constructive changes as it relates to the socio-political-economic status of the Mexican American.

Hispanic Urban Center. A community based educational institution founded to fulfill a specific need in teacher training.[6]

In-Service. A program of instruction designed to give cognitive knowledge regarding a specific or general area. As the expression related to this paper, in-service means a course developed for giving cognitive knowledge that may lead to the development of methods and techniques that will create behavioral change.

Mexican American. A person of Mexican descent residing in the United States.

Mexican American Community. An area within a larger community where the majority population is Mexican American. However, in referring to community as a people with a common interest, the definition is not limited to a geographical area, but tends to include all persons who may so identify themselves.

Program. A vehicle developed for the implementation of the course, The Mexican American in the Schools. Also included are the various experiences created relative to the course.

Syllabus. A summary outline of the course of study developed for the program, The Mexican American in the Schools.

Limitations to the Program

Most limiting of the various factors involved in this project was the premise on which the program was developed. No empirical evidence exists to support the concept that if a teacher has cognitive knowledge of a given culture the teacher will develop an awareness for individuals of that culture; that that awareness will result in the teacher developing methods and techniques that will improve the learning environment of a child from the selected culture; that this alternative methodology should lead to an improved level of achievement on the part of the pupil. Yet, legislation and major studies on the education of the Mexican American indicate this approach as one that should bring the desired change.

Another limitation was placing the responsibility for the development of The Mexican American in the Schools on the expertise of one individual. Admittedly there were guidelines, but once again, those guidelines tended to originate from an emotional community consensus rather than empirical evidence.

Initially the program was handicapped by the staff, which had no experience in this type of project. The staff tended to confront uncertainties more through intuition than cognition.

In consideration of its being applicable of a wider and diverse audience the program was confined by its being designed for the Los Angeles Unified Schools, consequently dealing with issues that might be common only to urban Los Angeles. On the other hand, this limitation may provide a point of comparison should the program be expanded into suburban or rural communities having high concentrations of Mexican American students.

The program being limited to the Los Angeles Unified Schools' staffs to a certain degree created a captive group of participants. Those school student participants enrolling in the program may have been motivated to do so to avoid community censure. Others may have joined in order to fulfill a requirement for professional advancement. Still others may have been actively seeking knowledge about the Mexican American youngsters in the classroom. There is no way to speculate on representative numbers for each of the groups.

The control group must be questioned not in terms of knowledge, but rather, as to whether it represented the Mexican American community. All the teacher candidates involved in the control group were part of a Ford Foundation Fund project that had as a requirement commitment to the Chicano Movement. Their responses to questions on the evaluative instrument can be assumed to be skewed to the socio-political-economic principles advocated by the Movement. The interpretation of these principles by the control group may be in opposition with those of the Mexican American community as a whole.

There are two restrictive factors in a complete evaluation of the effect of the program--time and money. The magnitude of the system where change is expected to take place impedes the measure of affective results. A corollary deterrent is the relative short life of the program--three years. Although measurement of change in behavior patterns can be made in several empirical ways, presently none is financially feasible to the Hispanic Urban Center. Despite all these limitations, the program has continued in its purpose.

Organization of the Study

This study of The Mexican American in the Schools is organized in the following form:

In order to provide a background on the education of the Mexican American in the California schools, a brief historical perspective is presented. Emphasis is given to several incidents that occurred between 1900-1970, not so much to underline the events as to demonstrate the attitudes that prevailed at various points in time regarding the education of the Mexican American. The chapter culminates with an introduction to recent legislation in the state mandating in-service programs for teachers on the history, culture, and current problems of a given minority. The law requires that such a program be offered wherever the school population is 25 percent or more of a given minority.

The third chapter of this study deals with the formation of the program. The issues that instigated the development are discussed. Included in this chapter is a comparison between the Hispanic Urban Center program and that required by the Education Code, Article 3.3 guidelines. The discrepancies between the two programs are presented. The settlement of the differences and the recognition of The Mexican American in the Schools as a prototype program for the implementation of Article 3.3 are also examined.

Chapter IV deals with the development of the program. The rationale underlying the design in analyzed.

In Chapter V, development and construction of the evaluation instrument is examined. Also, there is to be found in this chapter an analysis of the results for the first two groups of participants evaluated. Additionally, an analysis of the control group and the results of their responses to the items on the instrument is made.

The concluding chapter recaps the salient features of the study. The actualities dealing with the program are reviewed. Finally, speculation is made as to the limits and potentials of the project.

CHAPTER II

MEXICAN AMERICAN IN THE CALIFORNIA SCHOOLS

1900-1970: A BRIEF HISTORICAL PERSPECTIVE

Early Educational Neglect

From 1900 to 1960 the story of the child "of Mexican descent" in California schools was one not only of segregation but also of educational neglect. It is impossible to separate the stage, the segregated classroom, from the act, the performance of educational neglect. For the Mexican American child was further discriminated against by the teacher, who was occupied with teaching English to children who could speak only Spanish. These teachers operated on the premise that it was best to isolate the Mexican American student until he developed a proficiency in the English language. It was generally believed that to put non-English speaking students in classrooms with English-speaking students tended only to retard the progress of both groups. Such ways of prejudging the performance of students followed the philosophies and practices of teacher training institutions in the Southwest.

During the first decades of this century, concern for the education of the Mexican American was generally negative in its expression. The Mexican Americans were generally considered as outsiders. The various provisions made for the "Mexicans" to receive equal rights as citizens under the Treaty of Guadalupe Hidalgo had long been relegated to the archives of forgotten documents. Most attitudes as they concerned the Mexican American were shaded with demonstrable evidence of prejudice. Literature on the Mexican American student pointed out the shortcomings and inadequacies of these youngsters: the I. Q. scores on standardized tests were cited as proof that as a group, Mexican American children tended to be intellectually limited.[8] Such a limitation gave further justification for segregation.

More and more, the education of Mexican Americans came to be seen as the "Mexican problem." Stereotypic characteristics attached to the "Mexican problem" included being best suited for manual labor, finding it impossible to be on time, possessing questionable morals, inclined to be dirty, tending to be childlike, and having artistic predilections.[9]

Educators who proposed solutions to the "Mexican problem" were inclined to support the principle of segregation, as indicated by many of the Masters' theses accepted by Schools of Education of recognized California institutions of higher learning. In 1914, William McEwen at the University of Southern California wrote:

> Just so surely as Booker T. Washington is right in saying that
> Tuskegee and similar institutions are the ultimate solution of
> the Negro problem, so surely is the same kind of education the
> necessary basis on which to build a thorough and complete solu-
> tion of the Mexican problem. Like the Negro, the Mexicans are
> a child-race without the generations of civilization and culture
> back of them which support the people of the United States.[11]

The emigration of tens of thousands of Mexicans to the United States brought a new perspective to the "Mexican problem." The major historical events that transpired between 1910 and 1920 in the United States and Mexico, such as

World War I and the Mexican Revolution, brought mass migrations of Mexican nationals to the industrial areas of the United States. Accompanying these migrants were many rural Mexican Americans who saw new economic opportunities in the urban communities. California, because of its growing agricultural and commercial enterprises, became a magnet. This influx of Mexicans brought a greater awareness of the "Mexican problem." By the early '30s, educational writings such as that in the study of Charles Carpenter, who later became as assistant superintendent in the Los Angeles County schools, supported the developing stereotype as a factual characterization and recommended segregation. Carpenter, in his conclusions states:

> . . . (1) because of the great social differences of the two races, (2) because of the much higher percentage of contagious diseases, (3) because of the higher percentage of undesirable behavior characteristics, (4) because of much slower progress in school, (5) because of their much lower moral standard it would seem best that: 1. Wherever numbers permit, Mexican children be segregated, and that teachers especially qualified be placed in charge of Mexican groups. 2. [sic] A special course of study be prepared to meet the needs of Mexican children.[12]

The Depression brought forth a number of federal government projects that centered on a strong united effort to fight the fear that President Franklin D. Roosevelt had iterated: "The only thing we have to fear is fear itself."[13] These projects tended to emphasize cultural differences through their focus on "Americanization" and vocational education. Such projects gravitated towards those stereotypic characteristics that made the Mexican an outsider. The perception led to some educators seeing the school as an agency for the acculturation of the Mexican. In 1932, Betty Gould in her Master's thesis, "Methods of Teaching Mexicans," outlines appropriate methods for the Americanization of Mexicans. She pictures the school as the agent that would change ". . . Mexican children from half-hearted Americans into law abiding and useful American citizens."[14] A concomitant to this logic was segregation.

In his study of the four states bordering Mexico, Ward U. Leis found that in 1931, two-thirds of the school districts practiced segregation. His study indicates that the factors contributing to this practice were generally ". . . language handicap, lack of social adjustment, itinerancy and perhaps a difference in mentality." Leis recommends in the conclusion of his study: "The Mexican children should be segregated in their own buildings from kindergarten through third grade. This will require the abolishment of non-segregation acts such as that in the law of California."[15]

Katherine Meguire, in 1935, developed as her Master's project a handbook entitled Educating the Mexican Child in the Elementary School. This intent was developed for teachers working under the condition where even though ". . . segregation is unlawful, accidents of residence sometimes cause almost 100% Mexican enrollment." The booklet offered methods and techniques for dealing with the problems of teaching English to Mexican children and teaching the reading of English to Mexican children. Ms. Meguire recognized that "The Teachers of Mexican children have before them the enormous task of teaching reading in a language which is foreign to the children."[16] She also included a chapter on how to deal with the "racial traits" displayed by Mexican children. In this chapter she first recognized the positive qualities of the Mexican such as love of color and beauty as well as music and dance; additionally, she recommended that much handwork be provided them. The negative racial traits she implied through section headings such as "Develop a sense of responsibility; Promote initiative and self-dependence; Encourage thrift; Overcome self-

consciousness; Combat the individualistic trait; Overcome the tendency to procras-
tinate."[17]

As the decade progressed, schools in California emphasized for Mexican
Americans vocational and manual arts training, learning of English, health and
cleanliness. In those schools where segregation was not a community separation but
rather an in-school affair, the vocational and manual arts classes became the terminal
educational experience for vast numbers of Mexican Americans in the public schools.[18]

During the '40s, studies continued "to prove" Mexican Americans as mentally
inferior. In 1941, John S. Cornelius stated that his research proved that ". . .
intelligence of these pupils seems to be the most important limiting factor in their
learning." Therefore, Cornelius recommended ". . . that the kind and nature of the
subject matter which is taught them should be chosen with special care. The hand-
working artistic propensities of the pupils should be given a prominent consideration
in the building of curriculum."[19]

During the years of World War II, the movement from the rural communities
to the cities and their contiguous suburban areas accelerated. This new and sudden
growth often made for violent and bitter conflicts between the ethnic groups. Sharp
lines were drawn as to what was and was not American. These attitudes were in direct
contrast to the "Good Neighbor Policy" between the United States and the Latin
American countries. It was the Good Neighbor Policy that prompted C. C. Trillingham,
Superintendent of the Los Angeles County Schools in 1934 to outline a program for
ameliorating the conditions under which Mexican children were being educated. He
proposed a "Program of Teacher Training for Understanding the Cultural Background and
the Peculiar Problems of the Spanish Speaking." He also suggested: "Adjustments in
the Curriculum; Cooperation with the Home; Improved and Enlarged Programs of Counseling."[20] Dr. Trillingham concluded by asking a series of questions which clearly reflected his stance and that of the government: "What makes a democratic community?
Can we maintain the American way of life, if we do not live as friendly neighbors?
Can we build toward the promises of democracy if there is within our community an area
which breeds resentment and discouragement on the part of growing children?"[21]

Trillingham's type of attitude did prompt some changes. Here and there
appeared special schools which attempted to establish a democratic environment; however, most tended to be confined to Los Angeles County. Most efforts in the area of
"intercultural programs" were little more than token gestures of appreciation of the
Latin American cultural heritage.

The immediate post-war years saw a new resoluteness developing in the
Mexican American community for the creation of change. This perseverance was prompted
by community minded veterans who had enjoyed an unprecedented experience during the
war years free from bias, intolerance, and pre-conceived attitudes. These experiences
had metamorphosed the Mexican American veterans into an active group demanding change
in the status quo of Mexicans in California. The veterans formally organized; one
such force gave a new impetus to the League of Latin American Citizens.[22] The league
(LULAC) had been organized in the '20s having as its goal the development of educational programs; however, its effect had been somewhat limited. The commitment of the
veterans led to the formation of other groups seeking change in discriminatory institutions or practices, such as housing, public accommodations, law and welfare. All
the organizations in some way touched on the educational system in their communities.
The pressure for change was on. It was in this atmosphere that Gonzalo Mendez, et al,
as members of LULAC found themselves in the late winter of 1945.

8

On March 2, 1945, Gonzalo Mendez, William Guzman, Frank Palomino, Thomas Estrada, and Lorenzo Ramirez, as citizens of the United States and on behalf of their minor children and "some 5,000" persons similarly affected, all of Mexican or Latin descent, filed a class suit against the Westminster, Garden Grove, and El Modeno School Districts and the Santa Ana City Schools and their respective trustees and superintendents. All the school districts and the system were in Orange County, California. The complaint alleged a concerted policy and design of class discrimination against "persons of Mexican or Latin extraction" of elementary school age. This alleged class discrimination resulted in the denial of equal protection to the children of the complainants and "some 5,000" other children in the schools involved.[23]

The complaint stated that the school system and school districts involved did by common plan, design, and purpose, create "regulations, customs, and usage" which excluded children of Mexican or Latin descent from "attending, using, enjoying, and receiving benefits of the education, health, and recreation facilities of certain schools . . ." Allegedly the children of Mexican or Latin descent were segregated and required to attend and "use certain schools in said Districts and System reserved for and attended exclusively and solely by them. Children purportedly known as White or Anglo-Saxon attended schools maintained for their exclusive use."[24]

The petitioners claimed that the rules, regulations, customs, and usage were unconstitutional. They petitioned for an injunction that would declare the rules, regulations, customs, and usage void and that would restrain the defendant school authorities from further application of such rules, regulations, customs, and usage in order that their children be assured of equal protection and opportunity under the law.

As a result of the ensuing court decisions, Mexican American children were thereafter proclaimed not to be segregated because of their national or lingual descent. Although the decision of Mendez vs Westminster may have settled the issue of dejure segregation, it had little effect on de facto segregation. The Mexican American youngster continued to suffer neglect in the schools. The methods and techniques employed by teachers remained those learned at the teacher training institutions, or those methods and techniques generally accepted by veteran teachers, with years of experience, as being the most successful in dealing with the "Mexican"; therefore, their methodology was the one to be emulated by neophytes.

Yet, the 1950s saw a somewhat increased concern for the special education problems of the Mexican Americans. Educators conducted workshops and conferences;[26] these were serious and honest attempts by concerned professionals to instruct teachers in the cultural and socio-economic background of the Mexican American pupils. This information was generally oriented towards the teaching of English. The rationale was a recognition that Mexican Americans' attendance at school was poor, that their academic achievement was low. Therefore, it was indicated that there was a strong need to improve the socio-economic status of the Mexican American. The solution commonly offered was the attainment of the mastery of the English language.

Recent Development

The 1964 Orange County Conference on the Education of Spanish Speaking Children and Youth held in Garden Grove, California,[27] emphasized the need for special teacher training programs by the colleges and universities; the undemocratic character of the continuing de facto segregation; and, most important, the teaching of English. A change of curriculum or intercultural education was not underlined. Yet, there was a strong recommendation for the including of "cultural heritage" matter such as the celebration of Cinco de Mayo. Other materials developed for units of study tended to be equally stereotypic in concept and also quite irrelevant to the Mexican American way of life.

As the focus on civil rights and socio-economic problems grew in the 1950s and 1960s, the concern for the Mexican American started to rise. The tendency was to see Mexican Americans' problems as those typical of people of the low socio-economic status. This interpretation was given credence by the federal policies of the mid-sixties, developed to eliminate the conditions that created in the United States a substantial impoverished stratum. As one of the remedies, the Elementary and Secondary Education Act of 1965 provided an opportunity for the School Districts to develop programs that would compensate for those factors that created America's dis-advantaged. The term "disadvantaged" made poverty and cultural deprivation synonymous.

The orientation of compensatory educational programs for the Spanish speaking provided projects which promoted English language skills without cultural over-tones. Today, observers and evaluators of ESEA programs report that education programs relating to Mexican American children showed very few tangible results. The most discernible outcome of the ESEA Projects seems to be an increase in teachers' salaries and the acquisition of new school equipment.[28]

The motivating factor in these school programs generally seemed to be to im-plement the type of purpose expressed in 1950 by D. W. Brogan in The American Character:" [the function of the school]. . . is to teach Americanism, meaning not merely political and patriotic dogma, but the habits necessary to American life. . . the common language, common habits, common tolerances, a common political and national faith. The main achievement of the high schools and grammar schools is to bring together the young of all classes and all origins, to provide artificially the common background that in old, rural society is provided by tradition. . . "

The 1965 legislation triggered an increase in research regarding the Mexican American such as that of: Herschel T. Manuel, The Spanish Speaking Children of the Southwest--Their Education and Public Welfare; Uvaldo Palomares and Laverne C. Johnson, "Evaluation of Mexican American Pupils for Educable Mentally Retarded Classes"; Fred E. Romero, "A Study of Anglo American and Spanish American Culture Value Concepts and Their Significance in Secondary Education". Other examples are to be found in the literature of the period.[29]

The area probably most heavily studied was the academic achievement and I. Q. of the Mexican American student, especially as it compared to Blacks and Anglos.[30] Studies in the area of the language arts indicated that Mexican Americans achieved at a rate quite lower than the national norms.[31] The Mexican American child failed to reach a level of reading proficiency acquired by others.[32] It was also found that a Mexican American child's achievement in arithmetic was equally low; however, abilities in math fundamentals were higher than problem solving skills. It was generally agreed that the lag was due to language deficiency.

Additional studies indicated that there were other contributing causes for poor achievement in addition to language. Some were home-related factors such as: parental aspirations for pupils' educational attainment, pupil attitudes and values, language spoken at home, family economic level and so forth.[33]

The number and intensity of studies increased, most being based on an analysis of the 1950 and 1960 census data on the educational attainment of Mexican Americans. Included among these studies were those of Grebler, Moore, and Guzman, The Mexican American People and the California Industrial Relations Department's Californians of Spanish Surname.

More programs with the improvement of the achievement scores of Mexican students as primary objective continued to be developed. Few projects had an in-depth understanding or awareness of the variables resulting from cultural differences. The shortcomings of these programs are evidenced in the crowded files of ERIC, where scores of programs or projects repose without ever having been realized beyond the experimental stage.[34]

Interpretations of these findings were presented at the Hearings before the Special Sub-committee on Bilingual Education of the Committee on Labor and Public Welfare of the United States Senate, June 24 and July 21, 1967[35] and the Cabinet Committee Hearings for Mexican American Affairs held at El Paso, Texas, October 26-28, 1967.[36] The "Introduction" to the collected testimony of the hearings states: "The resulting composite picture formed by this testimony contains several basic themes. . . . Foremost in importance is the long acknowledged but long ignored cultural differences. Since . . . programs have been geared, in great measure toward the Anglo American population, the Mexican American has been left behind surrounded by all the implications that non-growth can have in a progressive industrial society."

Among most educators, the El Paso Cabinet Committee Hearings went quite unnoticed. However, within the Mexican American community, the lack of response by educators contributed to a growth in militancy, especially in California. The Mexican American militancy in California focused on education.

In March, 1968, several hundred Mexican American students walked out of their high schools in East Los Angeles. The walkouts were peaceful, orderly protests for educational programs based on the Mexican Americans' cultural identity and realities.[37]

The events that transpired from March, 1968 to 1970, including more student walkouts and a community sit-in at the Board Room of the Los Angeles Unified Schools, were aimed at the educational neglect of the Mexican American child in the schools of Los Angeles. These actions came in rapid succession.[38] They criticized I. Q. testing, de facto segregation, tracking, "special" curricula for the deprived, cultural exclusion, the "No Spanish" rule, materials with content that excluded the Mexican in reference as well as illustration, teacher attitudes, paucity of Mexican American administrators and teachers, the quality of the facilities, and other negative practices. Analysis of the criticism generally included an indictment against the schools. The schools had failed the Mexican through neglect and lack of recognition of their unique identity; therefore, the schools were responsible for the low achievement scores, the drop-out rates; the negative attitudes that tended to exist among Mexican youngsters for schools and for those that controlled them; the creation of an artificial school environment that pointed up some sort of "super-middle class"; the reinforcement of stereotypes; the development of negative self-images and so forth.

The criticisms were substantiated with facts acknowledged publicly, such as reading scores, average I. Q. scores for individual schools, percentage of drop-out per school, the disproportionate number of retardates among Mexican Americans (an issue that as this paper is being written, is still being contested; Los Angeles Times,

April 25, 1974), the unbelievably low enrollment of Mexican Americans in institutions of higher learning, the number of Mexican American youngsters involved with drugs and/or crime. Most accusations were aimed at those areas where the schools had assumed the responsibility through loco parentis.

The demonstrations became more newsworthy with the support of national political figures, such as Robert F. Kennedy, the return of professional and middle class Mexicans to their home communities and the willingness of Mexican American entertainers to identify with their barrio origins. Stronger focus was brought to bear as the Mexican labor movement in California under Cesar Chavez became involved in another struggle for civil rights. Generally, in California, the focus of the news shifted from the Black Movement to the new Chicano Movement as the actions of the Mexican Americans were now being called.

This ambience motivated changes relative to the I. Q. testing of elementary children; to the inequalities created in education by a fiscal system that determined the level of education by the amount of money a given community could raise through property taxes (Serrano vs Priest);[39] to the inclusion of special ethnic programs in most school curricula; to the development of ESL (English as a Second Language) programs; to the development of experimental bilingual programs; to the "special" inclusion of Mexican Americans at the administrative level of school districts; to the development of awareness for the Mexican American at the institutions of teacher preparation; to the development of special ethnic studies programs at the universities and colleges; to the development of special task forces within the California Department of Education that would deal with the unique problems of Mexican Americans; to the growth of Mexican American educators organizations; and to the development of community advisory groups for the schools.

It is in this setting that Wadie P. Deddeh, Assemblyman of the Seventy-seventh District introduced Assembly Bill 1117 (see Appendix A) dealing with teacher preparation. Assemblyman Deddeh premised his bill on the "lack of appreciation of a different culture [as] a fundamental psychological block to affect communication between teachers and pupils." His bill "was written to identify heavily [minority] impacted schools and require the personnel of that school to have some in-service training in the particular culture."[40]

In a letter dated April 23, 1973, Assemblyman Deddeh wrote:

We are saying that there are valid and worthwhile cultural patterns and attitudes among some of these groups that must be respected and understood, if successful education is to take place. . . . This has not happened with Mexican Americans in great numbers. It has not happened to American Indians. It has not happened to many of the Chinese children in San Francisco. Thus, in terms of state educational policy, we must try to meet the foreign culture half way. We probably cannot expect every teacher to learn Spanish, or Chinese, or an Indian dialect. But we can expect them to understand certain cultural attitudes, certain concepts that have different meanings in foreign cultures.[41]

CHAPTER III

FORMATION OF THE PROGRAM

A Community Decision

The Hispanic Urban Center had anticipated the bill offered by Assemblyman Wadie P. Deddeh by recognizing the need for in-service preparation for teachers on the history, culture, and current problems of the Mexican American and by designing an appropriate program to meet that need. That the Assemblyman had an independent motivation for advancing his legislation can be seen in his personal correspondence of April 23, 1973:

> I am both a former teacher in a school district with a large percentage of non-English-speaking children, and also a naturalized American citizen, having been born and raised in Iraq. It was thus apparent to me, both personally and professionally, that a lack of appreciation of a different culture is a fundamental psychological block to effect communication between teachers and pupils.[42]

To Mr. Deddeh, Assembly Bill 1117 was a way of establishing better lines of communication between teacher and pupil. Other statements in the letter suggest strongly that the legislator intended the legislation further as a means of erasing some of the conflicts that exist among the various ethnic groups and in this manner, possibly making the groups more acceptable to each other.[43]

The Hispanic Urban Center saw the program as an instrument for providing not only what Mr. Deddeh had indicated, but also as additional background for creating a greater awareness and sensitivity for the linguistic problems and the culture of the Mexican American. Through such awareness and sensitivity, teachers would be expected to create methods and techniques in keeping with the cultural differences and as a consequence to raise the achievement of the Mexican American student. This rationale is clearly presented in the statement of purpose in the syllabus that was developed for the program.

A. Purpose: To meet the needs of administrators and teachers of Mexican American students by:

1. Providing sociologic-cultural information that will lead to an understanding of cultural differences between the Mexican American and the dominant society.

2. Providing knowledge of the linguistic interferences that may occur when learning English skills.

3. Gaining information about Mexican culture that may contribute to the cultural differences between the Mexican American and the dominant society.

4. Studying some methods and techniques for achieving a more effective learning environment for the Mexican American student.

5. Investigating aspects of the community that will lead to a greater comprehension and awareness of the Mexican American community.

6. Understanding the differences among various groups within the Mexican American community.

7. Acquiring knowledge about the Mexican and Mexican American histories and heritages that should lead to the development of more meaningful curriculum and possibly more effective methods and techniques of teaching.

8. Analyzing problems and issues that directly affect the student in the classroom.[44]

The strongest motivating factor in the development of this program was unquestionably the abundance and consistency of data on the Mexican American student showing his low achievement and the lack of holding power of the schools. The annual reports coming from the various school districts regarding the achievement levels and the dropout rate of the students in the barrio schools were collectively presented by the United States Commission on Civil Rights dealing with nature and scope of educational opportunities for Mexican Americans in the public schools of the states of Arizona, California, Colorado, New Mexico, and Texas.

The specific appraisal leading to concern over the Mexican American student in California follows:

The reading achievement record of California students is poor to begin with and does not improve in the higher grades. In California, unlike other states, reading does not worsen appreciably as the children progress through school. However, a substantial percentage of children are reading below grade level as early as the fourth grade and they remain poor readers throughout their school careers. . . . 52 percent of Mexican American fourth graders are reading below grade level . . . . The general picture does not change appreciably by grade eight, but the proportion of those students whose reading difficulties have been allowed to grow from mild to severe increases substantially . . . . Upon graduation, 63 percent are reading below grade level and 39 percent have not advanced beyond the tenth grade in reading. Nearly one-quarter or 22 percent of twelfth grade Mexican American students in California are reading at the ninth grade level or lower . . . . Because California is the most populous of the five Southwestern states--with about 646,000 Mexican American students enrolled in public schools--this situation awakens particular concern. Such concern is heightened by the realization that an estimated 36 percent of Mexican Americans are gone by grade twelve because of low school holding power.[45]

Reading achievement levels have traditionally been viewed as the measure of determining school achievement, because reading is the skill most necessary for success and progress in academic areas. However, school holding power represents the degree of a school's effectiveness. In this area, the Commission on Civil Rights indicates that California schools have a better record of retaining Mexican Americans until the twelfth grade throughout the Southwest as a whole.

. . . even so, fewer than two out of every three Mexican American
students, or 64 percent, ever graduate. By the eighth grade, about
6 percent of Mexican American students have already left school . . . .
More striking than the percentage loss in California is the actual
number of students involved. . . of the approximately 330,000
Mexican American students in grades one through six, in 1968 about
120,000 or 36 percent [failed] to graduate from high school.[46]

Although the holding power of the school for the State of California figured
comparatively "better" among the Southwestern states, the local test scores presented
a negative level of achievement for the Mexican American. The Los Angeles Unified
Schools each spring since 1963, has presented a publication entitled Summary Report
Mandatory State Testing Program.[47] The East Los Angeles community carefully studied
the results presented in these documents. In a comparative study for the years 1962
through 1971, the community ascertained the consistent lack of achievement of the
Mexican American student.

An example of this comparison is excerpted here for the portion dealing with
reading of the third phase[48] of this state mandatory program from 1969-1972. The
scores here specified are for the sixth grade students in elementary schools of the
Los Angeles district having a Spanish surname enrollment of over 80 percent according
to the Racial and Ethnic Survey, Fall, 1972.[49]

National Norm Percentiles

School[50] Elementary	1969 %oile	1970 %oile	1971 %oile	1972 %oile	% Spanish Surname
Belvedere	32	37	34	37	96.9
Breed	46	39	33	30	93.5
Bridge	26	27	29	35	90.6
Brooklyn	25	27	27	28	98.5
Euclid	26	40	30	40	95.6
First	32	37	26	29	93.0
Ford	32	29	41	28	97.3
Fourth	35	33	40	32	91.4
Hammel	27	26	21	20	98.2
Humphreys	26	36	34	33	97.6
Lorena	37	34	27	34	95.5
Malabar	34	34	36	34	95.6
Marianna	25	34	27	25	99.1
Riggin	24	28	20	21	98.6
Rowan	30	30	28	30	96.8
Second	26	15	26	30	82.2
Sheridan	31	31	31	34	94.0
Soto	39	33	32	27	94.9

The above-named elementary schools are feeder schools to the high schools
indicated below. The following scores are for the first semester twelfth grade students in secondary schools of the Los Angeles district having a Spanish surname enrollment of over 80 percent according to the Racial and Ethnic Survey, Fall, 1972.[51]

School[52] High	1969 %oile	1970 %oile	1971 %oile	1972 %oile	% Spanish Surname
Garfield	43	46	40	38	94.9
Roosevelt	42	40	37	41	86.5

These statistical accounts spurred the community to action. The Mexican American community of East Los Angeles had already expressed dissatisfaction through the Mexican American Commission, the advisory group to the Board of Education of the Los Angeles Unified Schools, whose chairman was the Reverend Vahac Mardirosian. Having studied the various programs developed by the school district to improve achievement among Mexican American students, the community concluded that some of the programs had merit but all of them lacked the essential ingredient of understanding. The community's lack of satisfaction stemmed from the awareness that a program can be successful only if the one who implements it, brings to it a thorough understanding of the one who is to benefit from it. In most programs[53] no pre-service preparation regarding the Mexican American client had taken place: no teacher had been formally educated in the area of minority child development, that is, a childhood that had taken place in an environment sharply contrasting with that of the teacher's own. Therefore, rarely was the teacher able to adjust the program to provide for the cultural differences encountered in the classroom. The community as represented in the Mexican American Commission felt that regardless of the teacher's dedication and commitment, lack of a background mindful of the Chicano youngster handicapped that teacher; consequently, minimal success could be anticipated for both the teacher and the student.

The community, under the leadership of the Reverend Vahac Mardirosian, conceived the plan to develop the Hispanic Urban Center as an agency to provide the necessary enlightenment. The details regarding the constitution, the securing of the physical facilities and other matters dealing with the Hispanic Urban Center complex itself, do not have pertinence to this paper. Of direct relevance is the interest generated by the Hispanic Urban Center plan as it brought forth support from the business community of Los Angeles. The material and monetary contributions of the community were tangible demonstration of their belief in the potential success of the program. This support was further enhanced when the Department of Education of Occidental College granted the program academic recognition by offering four units of graduate credit to persons completing the course.

Additionally, financial assistance for maintaining the program came when The City of Los Angeles, East/Northeast Model Cities Program took the Center under its auspices. With the ever increasing pressure of community criticism and project acceptance, the Los Angeles City Schools agreed to cooperate with the endeavor of the Hispanic Urban Center.

Using federal funds gained from the East/Northeast Model Cities project, the Center purchased school staff time, consequently compensating these staff members for the hours involved in program participation. Those school people who took the course for credit relinquished rights to compensation.

Establishment of a Prototype

The launching of The Mexican American in the Schools project was concurrent with the amendation of Article 3.3, Section 13349 to the California Education Code.

The new addition to the Education Code mandated that:

> On and after July 1, 1974, each school with a substantial population
> of students of diverse ethnic backgrounds shall provide an in-
> service preparation program designed to prepare teachers and other
> professional school service personnel to understand and effectively
> relate to the history, culture, and current problems of these stu-
> dents and their environment. For purposes of this article a school
> shall be considered to have a substantial population of students of
> diverse ethnic backgrounds where 25 percent or more of all the stu-
> dents in the school are of diverse ethnic backgrounds (see Appendix B).

The development of the guidelines for the implementation of this law was assigned to the Bureau of Intergroup Relations in the State Department of Education by Wilson Riles, State Superintendent of Public Instruction. The Hispanic Urban Center offered a copy of its program to this bureau. Agents of the Bureau deemed the program as a model for other programs, incorporating much of its purpose and structure into their developing guidelines. The guidelines were formally intro- duced at two conferences meeting on April 27-28 at Oakland, and May 4-5 at Los Angeles. The conferences entitled, "Two Spring Conferences Relating to Diversity," were sponsored by the California State Department of Education and co-sponsored by the California Teachers Association and the Association of California School Administrators.[54] The co-sponsorship of the two latter organizations carried their tacit approval of the guidelines.

A detailed review of the guidelines by the Hispanic Urban Center staff was indicated when a single sheet summary prepared by the Bureau and circulated as ad- vance publicity disclosed a discrepancy of purpose between the guidelines and the Center's program.[55] According to this summary, the recommended format for programs designed to meet the law would be a preliminary course:

> . . . . dealing with concepts, themes, and issues including prejudice
> and discrimination, majority-minority relations, and the experience
> of various racial and ethnic groups in America; a second recommended
> course might focus on the history, culture, and current problems of
> one minority group.[56]

A study of the guidelines confirmed the summary description (see Appendix C). The guidelines recommended as a basic purpose the development of a program deal- ing more with effective than cognitive learning. The Hispanic Urban Center staff perceived the guidelines of the Bureau of Intergroup Relations as being in violation of the intent of the law in this recommendation. To make a formal stand regarding the discrepancy, the Chicano Caucus of the Conference Relating to Diversity was formed at the Los Angeles conference. The group requested a meeting with the director of the Bureau, Mr. Ples Griffin, and members of his staff to discuss the differences in interpretation.

The meeting was held May 17, 1973 at the Hispanic Urban Center. Prior to this meeting, the Caucus had dissolved itself and reassembled as a group representing the Chicano Coalition for Cultural Education, an organization which included repre- sentatives from various community groups.[57]

The Chicano Coalition presented Mr. Griffin with their interpretation of the law and a request for appropriate adjustments in the guidelines to accommodate the views of the Coalition. Mr. Griffin allowed that the interpretation given by the Hispanic Urban Center could indeed be more in keeping with the intent of the law; however, guidelines were not to be regarded as a set of rules and, therefore, school districts had flexibility in determining priorities.

The Chicano Coalition pressed the point that the CTA and ACSA co-sponsorship of the Conference tacitly gave the guidelines a rigidity not normally found in most guidelines. The Chicano Coalition further averred that the two co-sponsoring organizations had an insignificant minority membership and, consequently, could neither approve nor disapprove the propriety in matters dealing with ethnic minorities. The Coalition additionally affirmed their representative position as spokesmen for a majority of the Mexican American community. The community, charged the Coalition, was not interested in programs that dealt with a study of causes for prejudice and discrimination; rather, the community wanted a course that gave teachers knowledge about Chicanos. Such a course might aid teachers in their attempts to raise the achievement level of the Chicano child in his classroom.

The meeting with Mr. Griffin was followed by several contacts with Dr. Wilson Riles, Superintendent of Public Instruction, focusing on the controversy over the guidelines. A letter from Dr. David Lopez-Lee as spokesman for the Chicano Coalition dated May 18, 1973, emphasized to Dr. Riles his own words at the Oakland Conference: "If I had to choose between having teachers love my children or educate them, I would choose to have them educated."[57] The details of the correspondence and subsequent contacts do not illuminate the purpose of this paper. Of primary significance is the final acceptance of the Hispanic Urban Center Program as not only a proper program, but also a model program for achieving the intent of the law.[58]

A spin-off of such recognition was an invitation tendered the program developer in his capacity as an expert in in-service programs dealing with the Mexican American student.[59] The Bureau of Intergroup Relations of the California State Department of Education asked the program developer to participate in a staff development seminar. The seminar had as content the establishing of a cognitive background for evaluating the programs dealing with Mexican Americans developed by school districts for implementation of Article 3.3.

The acceptance of the Hispanic Urban Center Program by the State Department of Education as a prototype further established the program as potentially being one of the solutions to problems of lack of achievement and the dropping out by the Mexican American students in the schools of California. Of greater implication is the fact that the program was developed at the instigation of the community as the perceived the issue.

CHAPTER IV

DEVELOPMENT OF THE PROGRAM

The Guidelines

Development of the Program

It was the community who finally determined the content of the course, the texts to be used, the method of presentation. In this respect the program differed from most programs previously instituted with similar goals.

During the conceptual period, the Hispanic Urban Center staff and the program developer listed as their guideline the document issued by the directors of the Hispanic Urban Center. This document was developed by the Reverend Vahac Mardirosian, working closely with the community. On June 1, 1971, the Hispanic Urban Center stated through the document:

> This is a preliminary statement concerning a proposed program to provide in-service education for teachers of Spanish-speaking children in the Los Angeles metropolitan area.
>
> In undertaking this project, the Center seeks to provide a methodology of in-service education to teachers of Mexican American children that approaches the task from the sociological and cultural perspective of the Los Angeles barrios.
>
> Statistical analyses of the achievement of Spanish-speaking children in the schools of the Los Angeles district in the area of reading show that at the sixth grade level there is a two-and-one-half lag in comparison to the achievement of Anglo children attending schools in the same district. These conditions have existed for many years, and reading scores of Mexican American children have not improved despite large use of federal funds for "disadvantaged schools" in the area.
>
> We believe that an educational center in the barrio, independent of the school district, would more effectively train the teacher in the additional skills required to teach successfully in predominantly Spanish-speaking and economically poor communities. Our effort is predicated on the premise that it is the responsibility of the teacher to meet the level of the pupil, and not vice versa.
>
> The program of in-service education to be developed would include the following factors:
>
> 1. Linguistics. Teachers need to know, at least in a general way, the structure of the Spanish language and its relationship to English. An awareness of the phonology and syntax of Spanish would help the teacher understand the difficulties Spanish-speaking children encounter in expressing sounds

19

not found in their native language and in formulating
grammatically correct phrases and sentences in English.

2. Ethnocentrism. Teachers need to be aware of the extent
to which the majority society unintentionally imposes
its cultural patterns upon social and ethnic minorities
to the detriment of the latter. Knowledge of the economic inequality and social and political injustices
existing in the Mexican American community would provide
essential background for working effectively with our
children.

3. Mexican and Mexican American History. The attitudes that
some teachers possess have been shaped to a large extent
by a distorted image of Mexico and Mexicans, and by a lack
of awareness of the contributions people of Mexican descent
have made to the development of the Southwest.

4. Mexican American Values and Attitudes. Anglo teachers,
particularly those from suburban middle-class backgrounds,
generally lack familiarity with the values and attitudes
that influence the behavior of the Mexican American child
and his parents. The incongruence between persistent
rural values, transitional status of second generation
Mexican Americans, and the demands of the metropolitan
context often cause major maladjustments that teachers
must comprehend.

Other sociological and psychological factors similar to those briefly out-
lined above need to be considered by specialists preparing the in-service
educational program.

It is our conviction that a program such as we are envisioning would be
most effective in changing for the better the quality of the education
that is taking place in the barrios of Los Angeles.[60]

Based on this guideline, a concert of professors, community people, and
Hispanic Urban Center staff began to shape the program. It was concluded that the
program would take the following form:

The Hispanic Urban Center offers an in-service program to teachers
and administrators leading to a greater awareness, understanding,
and background for creating an effective learning environment for
Mexican American students.

Workshops

#100--The Mexican American in the Schools. The Mexican American in
the Schools is an in-service workshop designed to provide participants with information that will lead to a greater awareness of the
Mexican American youngsters' cultural and linguistic differences.
The experience is implemented through workshops of eighteen to
twenty teaching professionals studying, investigating, and dialoguing about various aspects of the cultural and language patterns of

the Mexican American with recognized experts from local colleges, universities, and the community.

The workshops meet for a period of several days for a comprehensive review and study of the Mexican American. This initial period is followed by a series of four group meetings during the period of one academic semester. These intermittent meetings are compulsory. They are designed to aid the participants in analyzing, reviewing their ongoing experiences in the schools. Methods and techniques for achieving a more effective learning environment are presented during the semester.

The participants are expected to be actively involved in a series of community activities that should broaden their understanding of the barrio.

Readings and recommended bibliographies are provided by the workshop leaders (see Appendix D).

This program as tentatively conceived by the Hispanic Urban Center was submitted as a proposal to the Los Angeles City Schools. On June 2, 1971, Superintendent William J. Johnston wrote these statements relative to the program:

> May I indicate the interest of the Los Angeles City Schools in the proposal of the Hispanic Urban Center to provide in-service education for teachers of Spanish-speaking children. I personally believe that such an in-service training program would be most beneficial to teachers and administrators through an increased understanding of the sociological and cultural factors of the Los Angeles barrios.

> . . . The District is committed to a new effort in staff development. We believe the Hispanic Urban Center could offer a critically needed component. We would like to discuss the details of a joint effort and then submit a recommendation to the Board of Education for its consideration.[61]

Dr. Johnston referred the materials relevant to The Mexican American in the Schools to the Reading Task Force a specially funded unit organized to raise the reading scores of pupils in forty schools in the Los Angeles area.

Twenty-two of the schools were predominantly Mexican American. Professionals involved in these twenty-two schools were the corresponding principals, reading coordinators, and 500 teachers.

The directive staff of the task force unit took the Hispanic Urban Center program under advisement. After study, the unit requested that the program become part of the Task Force's effort and set a beginning date of October 1, 1971. However, they insisted that the following become integral to the program:

1. Attitude Inventory

    Self pre- and post-evaluation to open-ended questions about participants' feelings and attitudes toward Mexicans and Mexican Americans.

II Culture

   Introduction (Overview of the Mexican American)

   A. Historical Background

      1. Pre-Columbian Period
      2. Spanish Rule and Its Influence on the Southwest
      3. The Age of Santa Ana
      4. Diaz Regime
      5. Revolution of 1910
      6. From 1910 to the Present

   B. Philosophical Implications

      1. How the Influence of History has Contributed to the Making of the Mexican American
      2. Difficulties of Assimilation
      3. Cultural Suppression of the Mexican American
      4. "Chicanismo"
      5. Priorities of Values

III Economic Conditions in the Barrio

   A. Rural vs Urban

   B. Mexican vs Mexican American

   C. Role of the Mexican American Woman

   D. Education (Family, School, Peers, etc.)

   E. Health

   F. Priorities of Values

IV Spanish-Speaking Student

   A. Castilian Spanish vs Mexican Spanish

   B. Language Differences (Spanish vs English)

   C. E. S. L.

   D. Communication with Home.[62]

The above content request with the tentative course outline was relayed to Dr. Ryf, Dean of Faculty at Occidental College, who, after consultation with his staff proposed that the College accept The Mexican American in the Schools as a four-unit graduate course. The stipulation was that the content requested by the Los Angeles City Schools' Reading Task Force be included in the final course of study. In response, the program developer made the necessary alterations and subsequently produced a syllabus which, at the same time that it met the specifications of the

School District and the College, remained faithful to the requisites of the community.

The Structure

The structure of the syllabus was a twenty-four page document that opened with a statement of purpose previously mentioned in this paper (p. 13). The statement of purpose was followed by listings of the various methods to be employed by the instructors. Methods of instruction included:

1. Presentations by resource persons

2. Field trips

3. Individual and group reading of recommended references

4. Group discussions

5. Analysis of reports and statistics

6. Presentation of films, film strips, sound tapes, and video tapes

7. Individual student reports

8. Evaluation (self-evaluation)

As previously stated, the community selected the texts to be used with the course. Their selections were specified as: A Mexican American Chronicle, by Rudy Acuna (American Book Company, New York, 1971); Mexican American in School: A History of Educational Neglect, by Thomas P. Carter (College Entrance Examination Board, New York, 1971); and A Forgotten American by Luis F. Hernandez (Anti-Defamation League by B'nai B'rith, New York, 1970). The final choice was Mexican Americans by Joan Moore and Alfredo Cuellar (Prentice Hall, Inc., Englewood Cliffs, 1970). The various sections of the course of study were keyed to specific pages within the selected texts that gave additional information or substantiated facts presented by the instructors or the guest speakers.

A rather detailed course outline that included the requirements of the syllabus succeeded the aforementioned details. These titles provided the framework for the syllabus.

I. Who is the Mexican American?

II. Stereotype of the Mexican American

III. The Mexican American and the Family

IV. Growth and Development of the Mexican American Child

V. Language and Language Differences

VI. The Barrio

VII. The Mexican American in the Schools

VIII. Contemporary Research in Terms of the Mexican American

IX. Contemporary Issues

X. Methods, Techniques, and Materials for Working with Parents, Home and Community.

XI. Historical and Cultural Sources

Each of the above areas of emphasis was amplified by a series of guide questions serving either to set the stage for the instructor or to provoke the student; further, these questions could be used as test items for the instructor to measure his success or for the student to determine his learning.

For the purpose of illustrating the format, the following sections are extracted from the syllabus:

1. Who is the Mexican American?

Readings: Acuna: pp. 2-9; Hernandez: pp. 7-16; Moore: pp. 6-9, 52-64, 71-74.

A. Definition of terms
B. Identification
C. Assimilation vs Acculturation
D. Contemporary Mexican: The Chicano Movement
E. Urban vs Rural Mexican American
F. Differences by United States locale
G. The Mexican National

Guide Questions:

1. Define the various labels used by "Mexican Americans" to themselves, e.g., Mexican, mejicano, latino, Mexican American,

2. Discuss how you identify a Mexican American in the classroom.

3. Illustrate the differences between assimilation and acculturation. Which of the two is implemented in the schools? Why?

4. Explain the Chicano Movement in terms of the community, the family, the schools. What are its positive aspects; its negative aspects?

5. Compare the urban Mexican American with the dominant society. Compare the urban Mexican with the rural Mexican American.

6. Why do New Mexicans consider themselves hispanos or Spanish Americans rather than Mexican Americans? Discuss how locale contributes to the differences among the various Mexican American groups.

7. Describe the differences that exist between Mexican nationals and Mexican Americans. What are some of the appelations used

barrio to identify the national? What problems does the national face in the schools?

IV. Growth and Development of the Mexican American Child

Readings: Acuna: pp. 120-124; Carter: pp. 7-33, 35-63; Hernandez: pp. 25-31.

A. Home
B. Community
C. Peers
D. School
E. Conflicts

Guide Questions:

1. What are some of the differences between a Mexican teenager and an Anglo-American teen-ager? What determines the differences?

2. Discuss some of the areas of conflict that a Mexican American youngster may have with his family.

3. Describe some of the activities that seem to bring Mexican Americans into groups or gangs. Why do they prefer these particular activities rather than those that Anglo-Americans tend to prefer?

4. Examine and discuss the pachuco of the 40's. How does the contemporary "gang" in the barrio differ from the pachuco? What ever happened to the pachucos?

5. Why do youngsters indulge in graffiti? Discuss some of the symbols to be found in it. Also discuss changes that are taking place in it. Discuss alternate methods of expression and identification.

6. Describe some of the marked differences among Mexican girls. Estimate causes for these differences. How are these differences reflected in the classroom? How can the teacher use these characteristics to her benefit?

7. How is the "drug scene" different in the Mexican American community from that in other communities?

8. What are the areas in which American youth seem to run afoul of the law?

9. Explain the bato loco in terms of the causes for his existence. Suggest methods for counseling and guiding these youngsters.

10. List the problems that seem to exist in the schools with Mexican American youngsters. Determine whether these are symptoms or problems. Trace the source of the problems.

11. Discuss some of the problems faced by the counselors and teachers in attempting to offer counsel or guidance to Mexican American youngsters. Determine the reasons for the difficulties involved. Offer some suggestions for the elimination of the obstacles involved in communication with the youngsters, with their families, etc.

VI. The Barrio

Readings: Acuna: pp. 145-151; Moore: pp. 109-118.

A. Geographical and historical development
B. Political groups
C. Educational issues groups
D. Social groups
E. Economic levels
F. Vocational opportunities
G. School vs barrio
H. Community agencies
I. Community opportunity agencies; Self-help programs
J. New cultural programs (aesthetic)
K. Health

Guide Questions:

1. Report on the history of the barrio in your community. How does it differ from that of the Black ghetto?

2. Research the development of political groups in the Mexican American community. Which are the most influential groups at present and what have been the issues they have supported or fought?

3. Give several reasons why Mexican Americans have not been successful politically. Analyze and discuss the various reasons you present. Offer corrective measures.

4. Discuss the educational crises in the Mexican American community from 1960 to the present. Discuss them in terms of issues, successes, and failures.

5. List various social groups of the Mexican American community. Determine their objectives.

6. Analyze the statistics dealing with income, employment, etc., that deal with Mexican Americans or Spanish-surnamed Americans.

7. List the various vocational opportunity agencies of the Mexican American community. What do they offer? Who sponsors them? How successful have they been?

8. Analyze all available statistics dealing with the education of the Mexican American, i.e., educational level, intelligence quotient, reading level, etc., for the last ten years.

9. Investigate various community agencies whose objectives are to assist people of the barrio with problems dealing with the law, welfare, immigration, etc. Estimate their effectiveness.

10. Make an inventory of cultural programs to be found within the barrio. Establish their sources of funding, objectives, activities. In general, make a comprehensive study of the programs, especially as they may offer assistance to the schools.

11. Describe the major health problems encountered in the barrio. Additionally, investigate the agencies that offer health aid to the people of the barrio; be able to describe their efforts and procedures.

An extensive bibliography completed the syllabus. It is important to note that all the bibliographical references were available to the students in the library of the Hispanic Urban Center.

The program was instituted with introductory seminar groups dealing with the identity of the Mexican American. A seminar group consisted of approximately twenty students. The groups supplied with syllabus and texts continued to meet for three hours, once each week, over a period of fifteen weeks. Interspersed among the seminars were field trips to various secluded or generally unfamiliar sections of East Los Angeles. The field trip groups generally consisted of no more than three adults with one teen-aged Mexican American youngster from the barrio as a guide. Other field trips took the participants to the General Hospital, to the judicial courts, to secondary schools, to community social functions. Some seminars were highlighted by guest speakers with expertise in such specific areas as the learning style of Mexican American pupils, language interferences in the Mexican American child, contemporary political, labor, welfare issues among various Mexican groups. Among those who qualified as experts were such people as: Dr. Manuel Ramirez, a clinical psychologist, noted researcher in the learning styles of Mexican American children; Ramiro Garcia, the Director of Title VII, Bilingual Program of the Los Angeles Unified Schools, a specialist in bilingual-bicultural education; Dr. Philip Montez, Regional Director of the United States Civil Rights Commission with broad experience in community relations; Dr. Ralph Guzman, a political scientist, co-author of The Mexican American People: The Nations Second Largest Minority; Robert Castro, director of El Proyecto del Barrio, a center for the rehabilitation of drug addicts.

An evaluation component was constructed to meet the exigencies of the Los Angeles School District, Occidental College and the East/Northeast Model Cities Program. This modification called for the development of an evaluative instrument, the adjustment of that instrument to meet necessary changes in the course and the identification and testing of control groups.

CHAPTER V

THE EVALUATION OF THE PROGRAM

Development of the Evaluative Instrument

The participants in the first four-semester-unit seminars were 158 principals, coordinators, and teachers from East Los Angeles elementary schools. One
seminar group was made up mainly of principals, assistant principals, and coordinators. The coordinator was a master teacher whose role was to implement and follow
through on a reading program that had been accepted by the Reading Task Force for his
particular school.

This twenty-member group was designated by the Hispanic Urban Center staff
for purposes of evaluation as the pilot group. To them was added the evaluator, Dr.
Richard Piper of the Southwest Regional Laboratory,[63] who had volunteered his services.

For the purpose of developing an evaluation instrument, Dr. Piper requested
the pilot group be launched two weeks in advance of the other seminar groups. The
instructor for the pilot group was to be the developer of the program. This initial
group would serve as a model to the seven seminar groups, consisting mostly of
teachers, that were expected to follow.

Dr. Piper hypothesized that the administrators and coordinators could be
asked to frame statements revealing their cognitive knowledge about Mexican American
pupils in the schools of East Los Angeles. At the first meeting, the pilot group
participants were asked to write freely for fifty minutes on the general topic: "The
problems you personally consider create the lack of achievement among Mexican American
pupils in the public schools of East Los Angeles."

From the written statements of the administrators and coordinators, Dr.
Piper induced that the participants isolated four major problem areas: education
problems, family problems, underemployment, community services.

The education problems gravitated to three categories: school related problems, learner related problems and home related problems. Distribution of the items
over the problem areas fell generally into this form:

      1. School Related Problems)--
          A. Services
          B. Curriculum
          C. Teachers

     II. Learner Related Problems)--   Educational Problems
          A. Symptoms
             1. Drop-out
             2. Achievement
          B. Causes   )--
             1. Alienation
             2. Health
             3. Entry skills
             4. Language

5. Self-discipline

III. Home Related Problems
    A. Educational status of parents
        1. Preparation
        2. Attitudes
    B. Study environment
    C. Moral support of child by parents

IV. Family Problems
    A. Acculturation
    B. Language
    C. Poverty
    D. Family management and organization

V. Underemployment Problems
    A. Causes related to the Mexican American
    B. Causes related to the employer

VI. Community Service Problems
    A. Politics
    B. Recreation
    C. Guidance
    D. Health
    E. Law enforcement

The instrument developed for pre- and post-testing the seven remaining seminars consisted of sixty-four statements stemming from the written discussions. The device was designed to allow respondents to estimate how widespread a given problem might be. There were five categories which specified a frequency band in terms of percentages going from low to high: 0-20 percent, 41-60 percent, 61-80 percent, 81-100 percent. The choice of five major response categories was chosen to correspond to recommendations for constructing Likert-type instruments (see Appendix E).

A sixth category, "Don't know," was added to the instrument to allow the respondent who lacked relevant experience or who felt threatened by a particular item to refrain from making a quantitative response.[64] This option was approved by Dr. Piper and the Hispanic Urban Center staff because they agreed that the socially sensitive nature of the inventory content tended to call for such an "out." It was understood that this reservation was contrary to the recommended procedure.

The items in the inventory followed the classifications stated above in outline form.[65] As an example, one item relating to school services under School Related Problems, read: "#63. Counseling for Mexican American at the high school level is inadequate." Under "Curriculum" in the same problem area, two typical statements included: "#44. The curriculum for the Mexican American child is relevant to his personal life and background"; and "#58. Mexican American children lose interest in school because there isn't enough for them to identify with."

In regard to the teacher and the School Related Problems, there were eight entries. Among them were the following statements: "#18. East Los Angeles school personnel understand and speak Spanish well"; "#48. East Los Angeles teachers think that Mexican American children are good learners"; "#10. The achievement problem for the Mexican American child lies in the conflict between his 'Mexican' values and middle-class values of his Anglo teachers."

In the problem area dealing with Learner Related Problems, the inventory items posed statements such as: "#8. Mexican American youth assume they won't get jobs even if they have a diploma"; "#23. Mexican American youth drop out of school to help support their families."

For a factor which may limit a child to poor achievement, item #6 read: "Bitterness and alienation inhibit the school achievement of Mexican American elementary school children." Another problem area, Home Related Problems, asked the teachers to assess these statements:

#39. There is an absence of educational tradition in Mexican families coming from rural Mexico.

#42. Mexican American parents lack sufficient educational background to help their children with school work.

#55. Mexican American parents see little value in education.

#36. Mexican American parents have a high level of aspiration for their children's education.

#46. Mexican American parents provide an adequate study environment at home.

These examples and other statements shown in Table 1 are keyed to the problem areas isolated by the East Los Angeles elementary school administrators and coordinators. In Table 2, the percentage of response per category for each item on pre-test and post-test is indicated. (Discussion of the results for the pre-test and post-test as made by Dr. Richard Piper is to be found in Appendix F). This presentation takes the form of item analyses. Dr. Piper limited his examination to the Education Problems for they were the most pertinent to The Mexican American in the Schools project.

The evaluation provided the answers for two major questions regarding the Hispanic Urban Center's course: (1) How well has the project done with respect to helping the student achieve the course objectives? (2) How can the project improve the course structure and content so as to make it a more effective instrument for achieving the objectives?

In response to the first question, it was found that learners did move in the direction of the course objectives. The forward movement from pre-test to post-test was slight, but it was consistent. The limited amount of change demonstrated that the course was on the "right track" but the emergent nature of the non-effective education of the Mexican American student demanded a more expansive change.

As to the second question, the data gathered from the evaluation instrument together with the observational information emanating from the staff members helped to alter and amend the course. The Hispanic Urban Center presented these recommendations for improvement:

1. Interpret the present general set of objectives in terms that will

30

TABLE I

DISTRIBUTION OF ITEMS OVER PROBLEM AREAS

I. EDUCATION PROBLEMS

    A. School Related
        1. Services (63)
        2. Curriculum (44, 58)
        3. Teachers (10, 17, 18, 26, 43, 48, 60, 62)
    B. Learner Related Problems
        1. Symptoms
            a. drop-out (8, 23, 51)
            b. achievement (30)
        2. Causes
            a. alienation (6)
            b. health (27)
            c. entry skills (57)
            d. language (50)
            e. self-discipline (52)
    C. Home Related Problems
        1. Educational Status of Parents
            a. preparation (39, 42)
            b. attitudes (55, 35, 36)
        2. Study Environment (46, 21)
        3. Parents Moral Support of Child (5, 40, 56, 4, 37, 28, 41)

II. FAMILY PROBLEMS
    A. Acculturation (29)
    B. Language (3)
    C. Poverty (12, 32, 38, 53, 54)
    D. Family Management and Organization (13, 19, 24, 59, 64)

III. UNDEREMPLOYMENT
    A. Causes in the Mexican American (7, 9, 11, 14, 31, 33, 34, 47)
    B. Causes in the Employer (22, 45)

IV. COMMUNITY SERVICES
    A. Politics (49)
    B. Recreation (1)
    C. Guidance (2)
    D. Health (15, 61)
    E. Law Enforcement (16, 20, 25)

TABLE 2

PERCENTAGE* OF RESPONSE PER CATEGORY FOR EACH ITEM ON PRE-TEST AND POST-TEST

CATEGORIES OF RESPONSE

ITEM	1 PRE	1 POST	2 PRE	2 POST	3 PRE	3 POST	4 PRE	4 POST	5 PRE	5 POST	6 PRE	6 POST
1	26	32	24	26	17	21	11	6	11	10	8	6
2	40	37	33	27	13	15	1	9	4	8	8	4
3	27	23	45	44	15	30	11	1	1	1	1	2
4	54	50	33	37	6	10	2	11	0	0	5	3
5	58	45	32	42	7	9	0	1	0	0	2	3
6	34	32	26	23	17	24	11	15	6	4	6	2
7	15	21	26	28	26	29	18	10	13	8	2	4
8	16	15	30	36	23	19	15	17	11	8	5	4
9	8	8	17	23	28	35	25	20	20	10	2	3
10	15	16	22	19	26	30	19	17	16	14	1	4
11	7	9	25	25	31	37	21	17	13	10	2	3
12	15	22	39	42	24	18	14	11	5	3	2	3
13	22	27	26	33	25	24	15	8	9	5	2	3
14	11	18	26	26	25	24	18	17	12	9	7	7
15	29	29	26	26	10	19	8	6	18	11	9	9
16	3	10	18	21	16	22	23	27	29	18	9	3
17	2	5	6	4	13	10	15	18	58	61	5	3
18	57	50	27	35	10	7	1	4	2	2	2	2
19	75	71	15	12	7	8	2	3	1	2	1	5
20	33	35	25	21	11	13	7	10	7	7	17	15
21	12	6	19	24	18	17	24	30	24	22	2	3
22	12	15	18	17	26	29	24	22	11	9	8	9
23	12	13	24	27	24	30	24	17	10	9	6	4
24	20	10	31	26	24	30	15	22	7	10	2	3
25	33	45	33	24	11	13	6	4	0	0	16	13
26	11	15	20	16	33	29	19	24	10	11	7	5
27	34	42	39	35	22	16	5	3	2	1	1	3
28	20	24	28	35	22	21	14	11	5	4	11	6
29	5	8	11	7	14	17	24	20	40	43	5	4
30	7	4	7	10	11	16	24	29	47	38	2	3
31	11	9	19	20	31	33	24	26	15	9	1	3
32	8	8	20	22	26	28	24	27	16	10	4	6
33	6	2	11	23	27	28	32	27	23	18	1	3
34	20	25	22	29	24	18	20	15	11	7	3	6
35	38	32	35	41	15	16	2	3	3	2	6	6
36	7	5	20	11	31	32	25	31	15	17	1	3
37	9	5	28	21	33	38	15	26	10	8	5	2
38	3	4	12	9	16	24	32	33	32	26	3	4
39	18	24	11	20	13	14	21	20	27	15	10	7
40	50	43	32	34	10	15	2	4	1	1	4	3
41	25	31	31	36	26	16	15	11	3	6	0	1

TABLE 2--Continued

ITEM	1		2		3		4		5		6	
	PRE	POST	PRE	POST	PRE	POST	PRE	POST	PRE	POST	PRE	POST
42	10	20	28	26	24	16	22	22	15	7	2	1
43	24	36	32	24	20	15	15	17	5	6	3	3
44	37	39	34	30	24	20	2	5	2	0	0	4
45	13	12	17	17	30	30	21	21	13	13	6	7
46	42	41	36	41	15	14	1	0	1	1	4	3
47	6	10	20	15	15	17	21	26	29	26	10	5
48	20	20	26	29	33	31	11	16	2	3	7	2
49	20	13	15	26	25	27	11	13	20	14	8	7
50	22	24	35	31	23	30	12	12	6	3	2	1
51	2	4	20	24	33	30	22	29	13	10	9	2
52	29	30	28	33	21	17	11	8	3	2	7	10
53	24	29	20	26	24	17	19	15	9	8	4	4
54	6	6	12	21	21	18	37	27	21	24	2	3
55	46	44	23	28	15	18	7	4	3	2	4	3
56	37	36	27	25	12	16	13	8	9	10	2	3
57	15	19	15	24	20	16	25	23	20	14	3	4
58	19	21	20	17	21	22	24	22	10	10	6	7
59	26	23	30	32	28	29	11	10	2	1	4	4
60	21	17	22	19	19	25	17	17	18	13	2	8
61	27	25	28	21	17	22	13	15	7	10	7	6
62	17	11	20	28	18	20	17	22	23	16	4	3
63	8	6	5	9	15	13	16	19	30	40	25	13
64	15	10	19	10	35	32	16	31	5	10	10	6

*Because of errors of rounding, not all rows sum to exactly 100%.

permit a more objective evaluation.

2. Develop a more valid set of evaluation techniques.

3. Develop and teach a set of criteria for curriculum developers that will guarantee relevance of curriculum to the Mexican American child.

4. Identify and teach those teacher behaviors which are facilitative of achievement in Mexican American children.

5. Identify and teach the specifics of the conflict between middle class American values and Mexican values.

6. Identify specific values in the Mexican educational tradition and the ways in which American schools can relate to these values.[66]

The Evaluation of the Program

The syllabus for The Mexican American in the Schools underwent a complete revision (see Appendix G). Portions of the document were submitted to experts in certain areas of emphasis, such as history of the Southwest, for sharper focus as determined by the objectives. Of the texts recommended in the revised syllabus, one was retained: Thomas P. Carter, The Mexican American in the Schools: A History of Educational Neglect, and two new ones were added: Rudolfo Acuna, Occupied America, and Carey McWilliams, North from Mexico.

It was necessary to revise the evaluative instrument in part for some of the items did not fit well into the test format. Others were ambiguous.

The Chicano Awareness Scale, as the test was now called (see Appendix H):

> . . . was modeled after the Dogmatism Scale. . . and the Inventory of Beliefs. . . . The theory behind items in this scale is the people possess beliefs that vary along the dimension of centrality. A belief that is truly central is one which, if it is changed, results in changes in beliefs, life style, expressed likes and dislikes, friendships, etc.

> To what degree do an Anglo American's beliefs about Mexican Americans affect his interaction with them? The presumption is that to the degree that beliefs are central, the effects are momentous. Is it possible for an Anglo American to hold beliefs about Mexican Americans which are subtly detrimental to relations between them? The answer is presumed to be 'yes.'

> Based on these assumptions, the text books used in the course were carefully searched for statements which indicated central differences in perspective between Anglo Americans and Mexican Americans. These statements became the raw material for scale items.[67]

Test validation was done through the empirical method of reference groups. The first people tested were mostly Anglo teachers. To make a comparison it was necessary to have a sample group who were expected to respond to the items in a positive way, that is, giving the answers anticipated as being "correct."

The test was administered to a sample group of Chicano students, members of Operation Chicano Teacher. Operation Chicano Teacher is a Ford Foundation Fund project at California State University, Northridge, whose members are being prepared to be teachers in barrio schools K through 12. If the comparison of the patterns of response between the two sampled groups were found to indicate a substantial difference, it could be assumed that the test was approaching the monolithic belief structures of the Anglo educators.

The revised test was administered to the 1972-1973 group of teachers who enrolled in The Mexican American in the Schools and to the students of Operation Chicano Teacher. Table 3 shows the comparison between the responses of the elementary teachers and the Chicano students in the O. C. T. project. The figures in Column 1 and 2 indicate pre-test and post-test item means on the 1 - 5 scale used by

34

the elementary teachers to indicate their degree of agreement with each of the various forty statements. Column 3 indicates the item means on the responses given by O. C. T. students.

Column 4 gives the scores of a group of teachers who did not participate in the program and who indicated that they had no intention to do so at any future time. The missing scores for various items exist because those items were not on the instrument used to test this group.

Dr. Piper states in his evaluation report for the year 1972-1973:

Insofar as it is possible to demonstrate with the Chicano Awareness Scale that a change in belief structure occurs, it can be said that the Center's Program is successful. There is a clear difference between the comparison and participant groups in their pattern of responses. The Fall participant group moved strongly in the direction of the Chicano point of view thus showing that at least they know what it is. Having this Chicano frame of reference can help the teachers deal more effectively with their children (see Appendix I).

As in all evaluations, alternative hypotheses must be considered. Of the two that relate to the program, one is that the sampling may have been biased in favor of the Center's program. Invitations to enroll in the Hispanic Urban Center's program had been extended to elementary school faculties on a voluntary basis on the assumption that those enrolling would become more favorably disposed. However, in some cases, there was the suggestion that subtle pressure had been applied by censure of the community or school administrator. This is a plausible contention, for in some schools nearly every faculty member enrolled while in others, fewer than half did.

The second alternative hypothesis that might tend to support sampling bias is the high percentage of participants that come from minority groups. Though most minority group members were not Chicano, there may still be a similarity of social experiences that predispose "norm" responses.

Despite these reservations, the evaluation did indicate success. It also indicates a need for study in the area of in-class teacher performance and the relation that performance has to altering the existing achievement score and drop out rate of the Mexican American student in the public schools.

TABLE 3

CHICANO AWARENESS SCALE: COMPARISON OF ITEM MEANS

Item	Column 1 Pre-test	Column 2 Post-test	Column 3 O. C. T.	Column 4 Comp. Gp.
1.	2.57	2.72	3.50	2.39
2.	2.25	2.91	3.63	1.47
3.	3.02	2.99	4.05	3.64
4.	3.41	3.67	4.18	3.21
5.	2.44	2.70	3.85	
6.	3.70	3.84	3.28	3.53
7.	3.41	3.28	4.25	
8.	2.91	3.34	4.38	2.38
9.	3.47	3.86	4.53	2.95
10.	3.34	3.72	4.05	3.03
11.	1.96	2.05	2.90	1.97
12.	2.06	2.45	2.33	1.92
13.	3.31	3.54	3.40	3.08
14.	3.53	3.61	4.38	3.50
15.	3.10	3.11	3.23	2.98
16.	3.60	3.81	3.95	3.21
17.	3.19	3.45	4.75	2.97
18.	3.35	3.59	4.13	3.09
19.	3.11	3.53	4.03	
20.	3.34	3.33	4.55	3.52
21.	3.12	3.29	4.50	2.71
22.	3.66	3.80	4.33	3.59
23.	3.52	3.62	3.35	
24.	3.02	3.16	4.25	2.95
25.	3.58	3.75	4.20	3.18
26.	3.36	3.53	4.30	
27.	3.29	3.35	4.30	
28.	3.41	3.73	4.48	3.03
29.	3.09	3.39	4.15	2.82
30.	2.78	3.20	4.10	2.27
31.	3.45	3.53	4.33	2.77
32.	3.41	3.63	3.98	3.18
33.	3.45	3.78	4.35	3.02
34.	2.97	3.31	4.10	2.29
35.	3.93	4.03	4.53	3.48
36.	3.79	3.87	4.45	
37.	3.62	3.86	4.58	3.11
38.	3.43	3.70	4.23	3.12
39.	3.76	3.87	4.75	
40.	3.52	3.52	4.03	3.02

CHAPTER VI

CONCLUSION

Summary

The central idea of this study has been to show that a community is capable of organizing an in-service program which assumes that cognitive knowledge may bring about increased learning for a given group of students. The Mexican American community of East Los Angeles, motivated by the persistent low achievement scores and high drop-out rate of its youth in the public school system, did estimate that the fault for the low level of achievement originated not in the students' lack of ability but, rather, from the teachers' lack of knowledge of the cultural differences among the students. A teacher unaware of these differences would find it difficult to develop the methods and techniques necessary for teaching Mexican American students the skills essential for performing at an appropriate level.

The descriptive study presents an historical perspective for the years 1900-1970, in order to establish the setting for this community action. The years 1900-1960 are marked by segregation and educational neglect; however, the decade from 1960-1970 saw a series of studies that supported the premise that culturally different children must be taught in terms of their respective culture they reflect rather than in terms of the culture they are expected to acquire.

The community of East Los Angeles, after having analyzed the data coming from the various mandated testing programs, concluded that the existing methods and techniques for teaching Mexican American youngsters were ineffective. Alternative methods of teaching and adjustments within the existing curricula had to be made if expected changes among Mexican American students were to take place.

For the barrio to create alterations within the system called for open criticism and accusations of incompetency. Such overt action would have the result of antagonizing the effectors of change--the teachers and administrators of the local schools. The pressure to be applied had instead to come from forces that were identifiable with the whole community, had academic acceptance, and possessed empirical validity. To achieve this goal, the East Los Angeles community established the Hispanic Urban Center with whole community support, secured the aegis of Occidental College, and prepared an in-service program based on the cumulative knowledge of recognized authorities.

The project utilized the resources of the East Los Angeles community to establish guidelines. From those guidelines, the program The Mexican American in the School evolved.

The program emphasized the culture, history, and current problems of the Mexican American. This emphasis proposed to give the school professional cognitive knowledge about the cultural differences, the historical background, and the contemporary issues and happenings within the barrios necessary to develop an awareness about the Mexican American. It was hypothesized that such knowledge would lead to curricular adjustments and the development of methods and techniques of teaching that were in keeping with the cultural differences of the Chicano student. The intent and content of the program elicited approval from the whole community, Occidental College, and funding agencies. The Los Angeles Unified Schools responded

37

to the pressures and also accepted the in-service training for teachers and administrators of schools within the greater barrio of Los Angeles. Within two years
several hundred teachers had completed the in-service training.

In the process of the development and establishment of the program, the
East Los Angeles community anticipated the implementation of state legislation that
mandated such development. The early production of the program contributed to its
identification as a prototype by the state agency responsible for the administration
of the law.

To assure meeting the objectives set by the community, the funding
agencies, Occidental College, and the Los Angeles Unified Schools, an evaluative
instrument was designed. This instrument, the Chicano Awareness Scale, consisted
of a pre- and post-test that measured the movement of the learner in the direction
of the course objectives. In addition, interpretation of the evaluation led to
improvement of the course structure and content for increased effectiveness in
achieving the objectives of the program.

Results of the evaluation demonstrated that the learners did move in the
expected direction. The forward movement from pre-test to post-test was significant.
This motion signified that the trainees had markedly gained cognitive knowledge
about the Mexican American.

Appraisal

The Mexican American in the Schools in-service program is a community's
attempt to solve a problem they perceived. That the program achieved its objective
of providing the school teaching personnel with cognitive knowledge is supported by
the results of the evaluation. Whether the knowledge gained will have a salutory
effect on learning by Mexican American youngsters is open for speculation. The cer-
tainties lie in long range and costly research.

A marked change in achievement by youngsters who have met limited success
for a number of years cannot be expected immediately because there are other variables that will create limitations, such as negative self-image, conditioned classroom behavior resulting from a reservoir of failure, peer pressures, and so forth.
The progress to better achievement can be characterized as slow for the youngster
who has been exposed to public school instruction through several grades. When
better achievement comes, it will be difficult to determine whether it is the result
of the efforts of one teacher, of a group of teachers, or possibly of additional
classroom help in the form of aides or tutors. Progress may also come in response
to forces outside of the classroom, such as changes of attitude within the community,
among the student's peers, within his family.

Assuming that there is a positive change in achievement scores, a study
must be made to determine the cause. Assuming the cause can be traced to a teacher,
or a group of teachers, then a study of the methods and techniques must follow.
Such factors are difficult to isolate; they are even more difficult to measure because of the limited control that can be imposed.

Of significance is the role played by the barrio community in developing
the concept of the in-service program, in securing whole community support for it,
in making the concept a reality, and in pressuring for acceptance of the program.

This effort by the community serves well to dispel the point of view held by many school administrators and teachers that the community is not caring and prefers not to be involved.

A spin-off of the Mexican American community's program was the insistence by the Black community for a similar program. Recently, funding was granted the Black community, by the East/Northeast Model Cities Program, for the establishment of a program dealing with the history, culture, and current problems of the Black. The program is housed in the Hispanic Urban Center.

Still another spin-off has been the utilization of the program's content to determine those competencies an individual must possess to teach in a barrio school. California State University at Northridge has presently an all-University committee working on the task of producing a list of required and recommended competencies. Potential teachers will have to give evidence of qualifications in such areas as: ability to recognize language interferences, knowledge of Mexican American history, understanding of social-political-economic issues in the Mexican American community.

One of the most significant outcomes of The Mexican American in the Schools program has been the evaluative instrument. This instrument's potential value as a screening device is considerable. The test could be administered to an individual who has indicated interest in becoming a teacher. The results on the Chicano Awareness Scale would indicate the beliefs the individual possesses about Mexican Americans. If the individual's scores are too divergent from what is designated as "norm," the person may possess beliefs which are subtly detrimental to relations with Mexican American students. It would then be proper to counsel this candidate to seek a position in an area having a minimum number of Mexican American students.

However, several parallel outcomes may tend to mitigate the positive results of the program. These outcomes involve the school district, the community and the program itself.

The program has not been institutionalized by the Los Angeles Unified Schools as part of staff development training. Institutionalization of the program would be expected to lead to a wider dissemination of cognitive knowledge about the Mexican American, a knowledge that the community views as benefiting its youth. Incorporation of this staff development project would contact a more diversified audience and provide added valid data for confirming the premise on which the project is based. Yet, the school district has shown a lack of desire to assume responsibility for the program. Participation has not been discouraged, possibly to avoid antagonizing the militant group of the community. The district's unilateral approach to staff development indicates to the community an authoritarian attitude in the seeking of solutions for issues that touch their youth.

With the lack of action by the school district, the voices of community criticism have been reduced in the direction of the schools. Some outspoken censors may be actively involved in managing, supporting or guiding the in-service program of the Hispanic Urban Center. Such involvement minimizes the efficacy of their criticism because of their closeness to the institution that will implement the expected changes resulting from the newly gained cognitive knowledge. The loss of outspoken community criticism may have the effect of misleading the school district into believing that its minority group oriented programs are fulfilling community expectations. Without mentor-type action from the community, the school may develop inadequate programs resulting in dissipation of funds.

The development of the Hispanic Urban Center has been the effort of a small leadership group within East Los Angeles. This leadership group in the past has been responsible for bringing about alterations in programs, policies and so forth that relate to the Mexican American community. Leaders have now been placed in a role parallel to that of administrators of the schools. Community activists are now occupied with budgetary issues, managerial concerns, personnel problems, and other administrative duties. This role has eliminated these necessary individuals from the ranks of active community citizens who are regularly seeking modification not only in the schools, but also among various public agencies in the community. Additionally, these new positions may have elevated the leaders to a level that separates them from the intimate contacts so essential for generating unified action.

The preoccupation of the Hispanic Urban Center leadership with managerial concerns has tended to stultify creative development of the program itself. The indicated expansion into areas beyond the "shallow" cognitive knowledge has not taken place. Expansion would develop for the teacher an in-depth reservoir facilitating effective methods and techniques for teaching the Mexican American. With full development of resources for the teacher in both cognitive and affective domains, the Mexican American student would benefit to the ideal extent of the purpose of the program.

The above four outcomes are further limitations generated by the evolution of the in-service program. Nevertheless, it is to be expected that as greater awareness develops for the Mexican American student, the need for teachers who are sensitive to the differences among these students will grow. The Mexican American in the Schools is a community effort to anticipate that need. The community has not implied in the development of the program that the teacher currently in a barrio school is incompetent. The indication is that the teacher is limited. The community believes that when the limitations are reduced, effective teaching of the Mexican American will take place in the schools.

FOOTNOTES

1. See Appendix G, p. 1.

2. Summary Report, Mandatory State Testing Program presented by Measurement and Evaluation Section of the Los Angeles Unified School District for Fall 1969 (Report No. 307); Fall 1970 (Report No. 315); Fall 1971 (Report No. 321); Fall 1972 (Report No. 329).

3. The program developer is Luis F. Hernandez, author of this study who personally observed most of what is recorded here.

4. Los Angeles Unified School District, Summer Report, Mandatory State Testing Program, Fall 1969, 1970, 1971, 1972, Los Angeles: Research and Evaluation Branch, Los Angeles Unified School District.

5. Barrio: name given by the Mexican American community to a district or districts where the majority of the population is Mexican or Mexican American descent.

6. Hispanic Urban Center: a community based educational institution. Definition originates from brochure published by the Hispanic Urban Center. Title of brochure ". . . nuestros minos no estan solo . . . ."

7. United States Commission on Civil Rights, Report VI, Towards Quality Education for Mexican Americans, pp. 211-212.

8. Charles C. Carpenter, "A Study of Segregation versus Non-Segregation of Mexican Children" (Master's Thesis, University of Southern California, 1935); Thomas P. Carter, Mexican Americans in School: A History of Educational Neglect, pp. 17, 21; William W. McEwen, "A Survey of the Mexican in Los Angeles" (Master's Thesis, University of Southern California, 1941); George I. Sanchez, "Concerning Segregation of Spanish Speaking Children in Public Schools" Inter-American Education Occasional Papers, No. 9, Austin; Simon Treff, "The Education of Mexican Children in Orange County" (Master's thesis University of Southern California, 1934).

9. Betty Gould, "Methods of Teaching Mexicans" (Master's Thesis, University of Southern California, 1932); Katherine H. Meguire, "Educating the Mexican Child in the Elementary School" (Master's Thesis, University of Southern California, 1938).

10. For further information see Master's Thesis Collection at: Claremont Graduate School, University of Southern California, and University of California at Los Angeles.

11. William W. McEwen, Ibid, p. 102.

12. Charles C. Carpenter, Ibid, p. 152.

13. First Inaugural Address given by President Franklin Delano Roosevelt, March 4, 1933.

41

14. Betty Gould, Ibid.

15. Ward W. Leis, "The Status of Education for Mexican American Children in Four Border States," (Master's Thesis, University of Southern California, 1931), p. 70.

16. Katherine H. Meguire, Ibid, pp. 36038, 40.

17. Ibid.

18. George I. Sanchez, Ibid.

19. John S. Cornelius, "The Effects of Certain Changes of Curriculum and Methods in School Achievement of Mexican Children in a Segregated School," (Master's Thesis, University of Southern California, 1941), p. 141.

20. C. C. Trillingham and Marie M. Hughes, "A Good-Neighbor Policy for Los Angeles County," California Journal for Secondary Education, October 1943, pp. 342-346.

21. Ibid, p. 346.

22. Leo Grebler, Joan W. Moore, and Ralph C. Guzman, The Mexican American People, pp. 543-545.

23. Paul J. McCormick, 64 F Supp. 545.

24. Ibid.

25. Ibid.

26. Thomas P. Carter, Ibid, p. 13.

27. Ibid.

28. See Educational Resources Information Center (ERIC) Annual Index, 1969-1971, Subject Index: Mexican American.

29. Benjamin Bloom, Allison Davis, and Robert Hess, Compensatory Education for Cultural Deprivation; California State Department of Education, A Report on Research and Teacher Education Projects for Disadvantaged Children, Project Description and Status; Walter Fogel, Education and Income of Mexican Americans in the Southwest; Robert Hayden "Spanish American in the Southwest: Life Style Patterns and Their Implications"; Celia Heller, Mexican American Youth at the Crossroads"; Robert MacMillan, A Study of the Effects of Socio-Economic Factors on the School Achievement of Spanish Speaking School Beginners; William Madsen, The Mexican American of South Texas; Joan W. Moore and Frank Mettlebach, Residential Segregation in the Urban Southwest; Robert A. Wenkert, A Comparative Description of School Youth, etc.

30. For example, Reports I-VI, Mexican American Education Study, A Report of the U. S. Commission on Civil Rights, April 1971 through February 1974.

31. Ibid.

32. Ibid.

33. State of California Department of Industrial Relations, Division of Fair Employment Practices, Californians of Spanish Surname.

34. See Educational Resources Information Center (ERIC) Annual Index, Subject Indes: Mexican American.

35. Committee on Labor and Public Welfare, Bilingual Education: Hearings before the Special Sub-Committee on Bilingual Education of the Committees on Labor and Public Welfare of the U. S. Senate, June 24 and July 21, 1967.

36. Inter-Agency Committee on Mexican American Affairs; The Mexican American: A New Focus on Opportunity: Testimony Presented at the Cabinet Hearings on Mexican American Affairs, p. 3.

37. Charles A. Ericksen, "Uprising in the Barrios" Educating the Mexican American, pp. 57-63.

38. Los Angeles Times, March 1968 through October 1970.

39. James E. Bruno, ed., Emerging Issues in Education: Policy Implications for the Schools, pp. 22, 52, 125, 127.

40. Letter from Wadie P. Deddeh, Assemblyman 77th District, to Ms. Ann Lane, Chairwoman, Education Task Force, Greater Los Angeles Urban Coalition, Dated: April 23, 1973.

41. Ibid.

42. Ibid.

43. Ibid.

44. Luis F. Hernandez, The Mexican American in the Schools: Syllabus, p. 2.

45. U. S. Commission on Civil Rights, Report II; Mexican American Education Study, The Unfinished Education, pp. 26-28.

46. Ibid, pp. 12, 14.

47. Los Angeles Unified Schools, Summary Reports Mandatory State Testing Program, Fall 1963-Fall 1972.

48. Los Angeles Unified Schools, Summary Reports Mandating State Testing Program, Fall 1969-Fall 1972.

49. Los Angeles City Schools, Racial and Ethnic Survey, Fall 1972, Report No. 327.

50. Grade 6: Comprehensive Tests of Basic Skills, Level 2, Form Q.

51. Los Angeles City Schools, Racial and Ethnic Survey, Ibid.

52. Grade 12, Iowa Tests of Educational Development, Form X-4, Test 3 (Language

Skills and Spelling), Test 4 (Arithmetic), and Test 5 (Reading).

53. All schools cited on p. 30 qualified for ESEA Title 1 funds, and other State or Federal Compensatory monies.

54. Memo dated February 9, 1973 to City, County and District Superintendents of Schools, from Wilson Riles, Superintendent of Public Instruction.

55. Brochure titled: "We Need to Relate" (brochure released by Bureau of Inter-Group Relations, California State Department of Education, Number 72-61 810-300 2-75 5M).

56. Ibid.

57. The Chicano Coalition for Cultural Education consisted of representatives from California State University at Dominguez Hills, Northridge, Los Angeles, University of Southern California; Association of Mexican American Educators; National Clients Council; PICA: Mexican American Education Commission; office of Urban Affairs, Los Angeles Board of Education, and so forth.

58. Letter from Dr. David Lopez-Lee, to Dr. Wilson Riles, Superintendent of Public Instruction, dated May 1973.

59. Letters from Frederic R. Gunsky, Bureau of Inter-Group Relations, to Luis F. Hernandez, December 21, 1973 and January 18, 1974.

60. Document: Hispanic Urban Center marked "Preliminary," dated June 1, 1974, initialed V. M.

61. Letter from William J. Johnston, Superintendent, Los Angeles Unified Schools to Reverend Vahac Mardirosian, dated June 2, 1971.

62. Document: from Los Angeles Unified School District, Office of the Deputy Superintendent--Reading Task Force, dated June 25, 1971.

63. Southwest Regional Laboratory, 4665 Lampson Avenue, Los Alamitos, California, 90720.

64. Hispanic Urban Center Evaluation Report, Program of In-Service Education for Teachers, July 10, 1972, p. 6.

65. Ibid., p. 6.

66. See Tables I, II, III.

67. See Appendix 1.

68. Hispanic Urban Center Evaluation Report, Program of In-Service Education for Teachers, 1972-1973, p. 3.

69. Ibid, p. 5.

BIBLIOGRAPHY

Bruno, James E., ed. Emerging Issues in Education: Policy Implications for the Schools. Massachusetts: Lexington Books, D. C. Heath and Company, 1972.

Cabrera, Y. Arturo. Emerging Faces: The Mexican Americans. W. C. Brown Company Publishers, Dubuque: 1971.

Carpenter, Charles C. "A Study of Segregation versus Non-Segregation of Mexican Children." (Master's Thesis, University of Southern California, 1935.)

Carter, Thomas P. Mexican Americans in School: A History of Educational Neglect. New York: College Entrance Examination Board, 1970.

Committee on Labor and Public Welfare. Bilingual Education Hearings before the Special Sub-committee on Labor and Public Welfare. United States Senate, Part 1 and 11, Washington, D.C.: U.S. Government Printing Office, 1967.

Cornelius, John S. "The Effects of Certain Changes on Curriculum and Methods in the School Achievement of Mexican Children in a Segregated School." (Master's Thesis, University of Southern California, 1941.)

Drury, Robert L., and Ray, Kenneth C. Principles of School Law. New York: Appleton-Century-Crofts, 1965.

Education U. S. A. Vol. 16, No. 22, January 28, 1974.

Gomez, Rudolph, ed. The Changing Mexican-American: A Reader. El Paso: Pruett, 1972.

Bould, Betty. "Methods of Teaching Mexicans." (Master's Thesis, University of Southern California, 1932.)

Grebler, Leo, Moore, Joan W., and Guzman, Ralph C. The Mexican American People. New York: The Free Press, 1970.

Griffith, Beatrice. American Me. Boston: Houghton Mifflin Company, 1947.

Hernandez, Luis F. The Mexican American in the Schools: An In-Service Program. Los Angeles: Hispanic Urban Center, 1971.

Hernandez, Norma G. "Variables Affecting Achievement of Middle School Mexican-American Student." Review of Educational Research, Vol. 43 No. 1, Winter, 1973.

Houts, Paul L., ed. "Education for the Spanish Speaking," (Special Edition). The National Elementary Teacher, Vol. L, No. 2, November 1970. Washington, D.C.: National Association of Elementary School Principals, 1970.

Inter-Agency Committee on Mexican American Affairs. The Mexican American, A New Focus on Opportunity: Testimony Presented at the Cabinet Committee Hearings on Mexican American Affairs. Washington, D.C.: Inter-Agency

Committee in Mexican American Affairs, 1967.

Leis, Ward W. "The Status of Education for Mexican Children in Four Border States." (Master's Thesis, University of Southern California, 1931.)

Litsinger, Dolores. The Challenge of Teaching Mexican American Students. New York: American Book Company, 1973.

Los Angeles Times, March 1945, February 1946, April 1947, January, February, March, 1974.

Los Angeles Unified Schools. Summary Report Mandatory State Testing Program, Fall 1969, Report No. 307. Los Angeles: Measurement and Evaluation Branch, Los Angeles Unified Schools, 1969.

Los Angeles Unified Schools. Summary Report, Mandatory State Testing Program, Fall 1970, Report No. 315. Los Angeles: Measurement and Evaluation Branch, Los Angeles Unified Schools, 1970.

Los Angeles Unified Schools. Summary Report, Mandatory State Testing Program, Fall, 1971, Report No. 321. Los Angeles: Measurement and Evaluation Branch, Los Angeles Unified Schools, 1971.

Los Angeles Unified Schools. Summary Report, Mandatory State Testing Program, Fall 1972, Report No. 328. Los Angeles: Measurement and Evaluation Branch, Los Angeles Unified Schools, 1972.

Los Angeles Unified Schools. Racial and Ethnic Survey, Fall 1972, Report No. 327. Los Angeles: Measurement and Evaluation Branch, Los Angeles Unified Schools, 1972.

McEwen, William W. "A Survey of the Mexican in Los Angeles." (Master's Thesis, University of Southern California, 1914.)

McWilliams, Carey. North from Mexico. New York: Greenwood Press, 1968.

McGuire, Katherine H. "Educating the Mexican Child in the Elementary School." (Master's Thesis, University of Southern California, 1938.)

Mendez et al vs Westminster et al, 64 Federal Supplement (64 F Supp. 544).

Salinas, Guadalupe. "Mexican Americans and the Desegregation of Schools in the Southwest." El Grito, Vol. IV: No. 4, Summer, 1971. Berkeley: Quinto Sol Publications.

Sanchez, George I. "Concerning Segregation of Spanish-Speaking Children in Public Schools." Inter-American Education Occasional Papers, No. 9. Austin: The University of Texas Press, December 1951.

Sheldon, W. H. "The Intelligence of Mexican Children." School and Society. Vol. 19, February, 1924.

State Department of Education. Directory of California, Superintendent of Schools, 1931-1948. Sacramento, Department of Education.

State Department of Education, Bureau of Inter-Group Relations, "Racial and Ethnic Survey," 1968, 1969, 1970, 1971. Sacramento: Department of Education.

State of California, Department of Industrial Relations. Californians of Spanish Surname. San Francisco: Division of Fair Employment Practices, May, 1974.

State Department of Education, Mexican American Research Project. Prospectus for Equitable Opportunities for Spanish-Speaking Children. Sacramento: California State Department of Education, 1967.

Stoddard, Ellwyn R. Mexican Americans. New York: Random House, 1973.

Treff, Simon. "The Education of Mexican Children in Orange County." (Master's Thesis, University of Southern California, 1934.)

Trillingham, C. C. and Hughes, Marie M. "A Good-Neighbor Policy for Los Angeles County." California Journal of Secondary Education. October 1943.

Tuck, Ruth D. Not with the Fist. New York: Harcourt Brace and Company, 1946.

Ulibarri, Horacio. Educational Needs of the Mexican American. New Mexico: ERIC Clearinghouse on Rural Education and Small Schools, 1968.

U. S. Commission on Civil Rights. Report 1: Ethnic Isolation of Mexican Americans in the Public Schools of the Southwest. Mexican American Education Study. Washington, D. C.: U. S. Government Printing Office, 1971.

United States Commission on Civil Rights, Mexican American Study. Report 1: Ethnic Isolation of Mexican Americans in the Public Schools of the Southwest. Washington, D. C.: U. S. Government Printing Office, April 1971.

United States Commission on Civil Rights, Mexican American Study. Report 11: The Unfinished Education, Washington, D. C.: U. S. Government Printing Office, October 1971.

United States Commission on Civil Rights, Mexican American Study. Report 111: The Excluded Student. Washington, D. C.: U. S. Government Printing Office, May 1972.

United States Commission on Civil Rights, Mexican American Study. Report IV: Mexican American Education in Texas: A Function of Wealth. Washington, D. C.: United States Government Printing Office, August 1972.

United States Commission on Civil Rights, Mexican American Study, Report V: Teachers and Students. Washington, D. C.: U. S. Government Printing Office, May 1973.

United States Commission on Civil Rights, Mexican American Study. Report VI: Toward Quality Education for Mexican Americans. Washington, C. C.: U. S. Government Printing Office, February 1974.

Wagner, Nathaniel N. and Marsha J. Haug. Chicanos: Social and Psychological Perspectives. St. Louis: The C. V. Mosby Company, 1971.

Westminster School District of Orange County et al versus Mendez et al, 161
Federal Reporter, 2nd Series.   (161F 2d 774).

ASSEMBLY BILL NO. 1117

CHAPTER 1586

An act to add Article 2.7 (commencing with Section 13250) to Chapter 2 of Division 10 of the Education Code, relating to teachers.

[Approved by Governor September 4, 1969. Filed with Secretary of State September 6, 1969.]

The people of the State of California do enact as follows:

SECTION 1. Article 2.7 (commencing with Section 13250) is added to Chapter 2 of Division 10 of the Education Code, to read:

Article 2.7. Teacher Preparation

13250. On and after July 1, 1974, each school with a substantial population of students of diverse ethnic backgrounds shall provide an in-service preparation program designed to prepare teachers and other professional school service personnel to understand and effectively relate to the history, culture, and current problems of these students and their environment. For purposes of this article a school shall be considered to have a substantial population of students of diverse ethnic backgrounds where 25 percent or more of all the students in the school are of diverse ethnic backgrounds.

13250. 1. The Department of Education shall develop a list of approved courses which shall be considered acceptable for meeting the requirements of this article. The department shall cause a list of approved courses to be published and distributed to interested teachers, administrators, and governing boards of school districts. The department shall be responsible for coordinating the efforts of school districts and colleges to develop adequate course offerings to satisfy the requirements of this article.

13250.2. In-service programs designed to fulfill the requirements of this article may include, but need not be limited to, courses offered by community colleges and colleges and universities approved by the State Board of Education. A district may provide an in-service program consisting in whole or in part of preparation other than college courses.

Such a program shall be developed cooperatively with the Department of Education and shall have prior approval of the Department of Education. An in-service program which meets the intent of this article shall encompass the history, culture, and current problems of the students of diverse ethnic background.

All college courses approved by the Department of Education for the purposes of this article shall be considered acceptable for salary credit purposes by any school district. District in-service programs shall specify an amount of equivalent credit which shall be acceptable for salary credit purposes in the school district providing the in-service program.

13250.3.   The Department of Education shall provide in its budget for the necessary funds to employ appropriate staff to implement the intent of this article.

13250.4.   The Department of Education shall make a progress report to the Legislature not later than the fifth legislative day of the 1972 Regular Session. The department shall further report not later than the fifth legislative day of the 1974 Regular Session the number of districts to which this article is applicable at that time and the extent to which implementation has been achieved.   The department shall continually evaluate the results of this article.

APPENDIX B

EDUCATION CODE, ARTICLE 3.3.

SECTIONS 13345-13349

Article 3.3 Teacher Preparation

(Heading of Article 3.3 added by renumbering

Article 2.7 by Stats. 1971, Ch. 438)

In-Service Preparation in Ethnic Backgrounds

13345. On and after July 1, 1974, each school with a substantial population of students of diverse ethnic backgrounds shall provide an in-service preparation program designed to prepare teachers and other professional school service personnel to understand and effectively relate to the history, culture, and current problems of these students and their environment. For purposes of this article a school shall be considered to have a substantial population of students of diverse ethnic backgrounds where 25 percent or more of all the students in the school are of diverse ethnic backgrounds.

(Added by renumbering Section 13250, as added by Stats. 1969, Ch. 1586, by Stats. 1971, Ch. 438. See also section of same number added to Article 3.5 by Stats. 1971, Ch. 1654.)

Approved Courses

13346. The Department of Education shall develop a list of approved courses which shall be considered acceptable for meeting the requirements of this article. The department shall cause a list of approved courses to be published and distributed to interested teachers, administrators, and governing boards of school districts. The department shall be responsible for coordinating the efforts of school districts and colleges to develop adequate course offerings to satisfy the requirements of this article.

(Added by renumbering Section 13250.1 by Stats. 1971, Ch. 438. See also section of same number added to Article 3.5 by Stats. 1971, Ch. 1654.)

Content of In-Service Programs

13347. In-service programs designed to fulfill the requirements of this article may include, but need not be limited to, courses offered by community colleges and colleges and universities approved by the State Board of Education. A district may provide an in-service program consisting in whole or in part of preparation other than college courses.

Such a program shall be developed cooperatively with the Department of Education and shall have prior approval of the Department of Education. An in-service program which meets the intent of this article shall encompass the history, culture, and current problems of the students of diverse ethnic background.

All college courses approved by the Department of Education for the purposes of this article shall be considered acceptable for salary credit purposes by any school district. District in-service programs shall specify an amount of equivalent credit which shall be acceptable for salary credit purposes in the school district providing the in-service program.

(Added by renumbering Section 13250.2, as added by Stats. 1969, Ch. 1586, by Stats. 1971, Ch. 438.)

Budget

13348. The Department of Education shall provide in its budget for the necessary funds to employ appropriate staff to implement the intent of this article.

(Added by renumbering Section 13250.3 by Stats. 1971, Ch. 438.)

Report to Legislature

13349. The Department of Education shall make a progress report to the Legislature not later than the fifth legislative day of the 1972 Regular Session. The department shall further report not later than the fifth legislative day of the 1974 Regular Session the number of districts to which this article is applicable at that time and the extent to which implementation has been achieved. The department shall continually evaluate the results of this article.

(Added by renumbering Section 13250.4, as added by Stats. 1969, Ch. 1586, by Stats. 1971, Ch. 439.)

APPENDIX C

SCHOOL STAFF PREPARATION IN THE HISTORY,

CULTURE, AND CURRENT PROBLEMS OF

RACIAL AND ETHNIC MINORITIES

Guidelines

1.0 GENERAL

Education Code Sections 13344 through 13344.4 (Article 3.3 of Chapter 2 of Division 10) state that by July 1, 1974, each California public school in which 25 percent or more of the students are of diverse ethnic backgrounds shall provide an in-service program designed to prepare teachers and other professional school service personnel to understand and effectively relate to the history, culture, and current problems of these students and their environment. The primary responsibility is that of the local school district to plan, conduct, and evaluate the in-service program and to encourage maximum participation by school staff. Sections 13344.1, 13344.3, and 13344.4 require the State Department of Education to perform the following functions:

a. Develop a list of approved college courses and distribute it to teachers, administrators, and governing boards of school districts. The Department also is directed to coordinate the efforts of school districts and colleges to develop adequate course offerings;

b. Cooperate with school districts in developing in-service programs in minority and other ethnic backgrounds and approve such programs prior to implementation;

c. Make progress reports, including one in 1974 on the number of districts to which the code sections are applicable at that time and of the extent to which implementation has been achieved;

d. Continually evaluate the results of in-service programs in the history, culture, and current problems of minority groups;

e. Provide in the Department budget for the necessary funds to employ appropriate staff to fulfill the Department's responsibilities with respect to these programs.

1.1 Participating schools

For the purpose of determining which schools are required to provide the programs described in Article 3.3, the Department of Education has applied the definition of racial and ethnic minority groups utilized in its surveys and those of other State and Federal agencies. The groups counted are: American Indian, Black, Asian, Filipino and other non-white, Spanish- and Portuguese-surnamed.

Data from the 1971-72 racial and ethnic survey of California public schools indicate that 2,670 elementary and secondary schools, or more than one-third of all public schools in the state, have reported that 25 percent or more of their students are members of minority groups. Located in 47 of California's 58 counties, these schools are administered by 471 school districts. Although 163 of the 2,670 schools identified are small rural schools with fewer than 100 students each, nearly one-third (827 schools) are located in the state's 12 largest school districts. There are fifty-four districts in which 10 or more schools are required to participate in these in-service programs.

Students attending the 2,670 schools comprise 39.7 percent of all students in the state. The group includes 90.1 percent of all of California's Black students and 72.9 percent of all of California's Spanish-surnamed students. The racial and ethnic composition of the identified schools is as follows:

Racial/Ethnic Group	Number of Students	Percent of Total	Number of Professional Staff	Percent of Total
American Indian	6,827	.4	129	.2
Black	374,154	21.6	9,179	11.2
Asian	63,429	3.7	2,672	3.3
Filipino/Other Non-white	24,519	1.4	499	.6
Spanish-Surnamed	506,748	29.3	3,444	4.2
Other White	753,395	43.6	65,836	80.5

1.2 Definitions

1.2.1 An ethnic background is defined as the collective experience and group identification transmitted by families and communities with a common heritage of history, national origin, cultural tradition, language, or religion.

1.2.2 Minority groups are defined as including the following: American Indian, Black Asian, Filipino, Other Non-white, Spanish-and Portuguese-surnamed. The minority groups named are of diverse ethnic backgrounds, and it is students of those groups who are to be counted to determine whether a school is required to provide an in-service program. Course content may include, in addition, the history, culture, and current problems of students in the district who are of other ethnic backgrounds.

1.3 Participating Districts

Each school district with one or more schools in which 25 percent or more of the students are members of minority groups must:

a. Design a program of in-service preparation in the history, culture, and current problems of minority and ethnic groups;

b. Submit program plans to the Department of Education for approval and obtain such approval prior to implementation;

c. Participate in coordinated efforts with colleges to develop adequate course offerings;

d. Carry out the program as approved, evaluate it, and make required reports to the Department of Education.

1.4 Goals of a District Program

An in-service preparation program meeting the requirements of Article 3.3 will include courses, conducted either by school districts or by colleges and universities, which offer information and learning experiences regarding the history, culture, and current problems of students of diverse ethnic backgrounds and their environment in order to improve the ability of staff to provide relevant and effective instruction in schools with 25 to 100 percent minority enrollment.

The Department of Education has established the following additional goals for these in-service programs.

a. To develop respect for minority-group cultural traditions and for the aspirations of minority-group children and families;

b. To develop understanding of special problems of learning and behavior in schools of mixed or predominantly minority racial and ethnic composition;

c. To help teachers and other school staff to improve the quality of their relationships with students and to improve the quality of relationships among students of diverse racial, ethnic, national origin, cultural and religious heritage;

d. To promote higher expectations of educational achievement and of career and vocational preparation by minority-group students;

e. To increase knowledge of available resources and of instructional strategies appropriate to schools of mixed or predominantly minority racial and ethnic composition.

1.1.1 Objectives used by school districts in the evaluation of outcomes of component courses in these programs are expected to reflect the goals stated in Section 1.4.

1.5 Suggested Curriculum

Schools covered by the requirements of Article 3.3 have been defined as those reporting 25 percent or more student enrollment in the following racial and ethnic categories: American Indian, Asian, Black, Filipino, Other Non-white, Spanish- and Portuguese-surnamed. In planning in-service courses and programs, school districts should emphasize the history, culture, and current problems of those groups. They should also take cognizance of the history, culture, and current problems of the students of other ethnic backgrounds in the district. It is expected that in-service courses will give attention to the sources of prejudice, discrimination and conflict relating to any of the diverse groups in the public schools.

1.5.1 Specific concepts and historical developments to be taught in in-service courses may include:

    a. Concepts of culture

        (1) Social and psychological factors in the development of culture

        (2) Effects on personality and perception

        (3) Value systems: norms, beliefs, behavior

        (4) Unity and diversity in cultural patterns

        (5) Dynamics of change

        (6) Cultural institutions

        (7) Race, ethnicity, nationality, religion

    b. Themes and issues in American history

        (1) Development of "minority" and "majority" groups in the United States

        (2) The melting pot versus cultural pluralism

        (3) Distribution and utilization of power

        (4) Distribution of poverty and affluence

    c. Effects of discrimination on racial, ethnic, national origin, cultural, and religious groups in American society

        (1) Institutional aspects: Schools, governments and legal systems, news media, business and economy, religion, arts, and community activities, public services

        (2) Interpersonal aspects: Stereotyping, avoidance, discrimination, physical attack and genocide

1.5.2 After the introduction of concepts, themes, and issues, it is essential to apply this body of knowledge to the school and classroom through participation in field assignments or similar experiences to allow for interaction with racial and ethnic groups from the community served by the school. Here the courses should provide realistic learning activities related to the following:

a. Definitions of equal education as related to the school and classroom;

b. Assessments of students' abilities and achievements;

c. Differences in students' learning styles;

d. Teacher, family, and societal expectations of students;

e. Self-image of students;

f. Concepts of desegregation, integration, pluralism as related to the school and classroom;

g. Role models;

h. Experience in the wider community, including observation of community organizations and how they function;

i. Militancy and activism in the community;

j. Conflict between different minority and ethnic groups;

k. Structure and governance of schools;

l. Curriculum and instructional materials;

m. Communication modes and skills of students;

n. Self-image assessment of participants with particular reference to intergroup concerns;

o. Observation of successful teachers and their methods.

1.6 Recommended Format and Techniques

In designing a program to meet the requirements of Article 3.3, a school district or cooperating districts may select from among a number of different formats and a variety of methods of instruction. The following, based on experience and discussion, are recommended for consideration among others:

a. A basic course introducing the concepts, themes and issues listed in Section 1.5.1 of these guidelines, with illustrations and examples from the history, culture, and current problems of many minority and ethnic groups. This would be followed by courses relating to the history, culture, and current problems of each of the particular minority and ethnic groups which predominate in the student population of each school, including the components listed in Section 1.5.2;

b. A course for teams from participating schools throughout the district, followed by instruction by the team at each school site. This basic course would be followed by other, more specialized courses or activities relating to each of those minority and ethnic groups which predominate in the student population of the school;

c. In districts where many schools have concentrations of the same minority or ethnic group, a comprehensive course or courses developed at a center or college which include basic concepts, themes, and issues, but explores in depth the history, culture, and current problems of that group;

d. In any of the above, various methods of instruction may be used, including workshops, seminars, lectures, and panel presentations, field visits and interviews, individual projects, classroom demonstrations, readings, written reports and papers, films and other audio-visual media, role playing, and dramatic and other performances;

e. Emphasis should be placed on practical, realistic approaches to meeting the educational needs of children in mixed or predominantly minority classrooms. Those methods are preferred which provide first-hand experience with minority-group people and their environment;

f. Minority- and ethnic-group parents, community representatives, and older students are a valuable resource in these courses, given prior briefing and training. It is recommended that maximum use be made of members of minority and ethnic groups as presenters;

g. The plan should provide each teacher or other member of school staff with a total program of at least 60 to 90 hours of instruction and other activities (equivalent to 4 to 6 semester-units for credit purposes). When a school has a large number of students in each of two minority or ethnic groups, specialized courses in the history, culture, and current problems of each group should be provided, and staff should be encouraged to participate in both courses.

1.7 College and University Courses

In-service teacher preparation programs, according to Section 13344.2, may include, but need not be limited to, courses offered by community colleges and other colleges and universities. A district may provide an in-service program consisting in whole or in part of preparation other than college courses. A college course, to be included in a district program, must be approved by the State Department of Education.

Because the scope of appropriate programs includes three elements, the history, the culture, and the current problems of those minority and ethnic groups present among the students in participating schools, some college and university courses with a specialized focus or emphasis may not qualify for approval. Section 13346 holds the Department of Education responsible for coordinating the efforts of school districts and colleges to develop adequate course offerings to satisfy the requirements. It appears that further course development will be necessary.

Experience will show to what extent the colleges can provide courses to meet the needs of districts in these programs. Districts in different areas will have different needs, and the resources of the colleges will vary. What is contemplated is a partnership between colleges and school districts, with the latter determining the program pattern which is best for each of them.

1.8 <u>Schedules for Implementation</u>

The requirement of implementation on and after July 1, 1974, in a statute enacted in 1969, recognizes a need for program development over time. The Department of Education proposes initial implementation of programs under these guidelines during school year 1973-74, and completion of course work by school staff, to the extent that is feasible, by the end of school year 1975-76. Thereafter, district programs should continue to provide for the in-service preparation of staff newly assigned to participating schools.

1.8.1 The Department of Education will establish procedures for submittal, review, and approval of district program plans. Review panels will include representatives of the minority groups concerned and of teachers and other school staff.

1.8.2 Following is the Department's schedule for action on district program plans:

a. By December 31, 1973, submission of district program plans for Department approval;

b. By January 31, 1974, notice of approval to each district (unless modification of the plan is indicated);

c. By June 30, 1974, and each June 30 thereafter, submission of district evaluation reports and proposed program changes to be approved by the Department.

1.8.3 The Department of Education and the colleges and universities will establish procedures for submittal, review and approval of college courses. Following is the Department's schedule for action on college courses:

a. By June 30, 1973, submission of college course plans for Department approval;

b. By September 15, 1973, notice of approval to each college, and publication of the first list of approved college courses;

c. At the end of each year thereafter, publication of new and revised lists as additional course plans are submitted and approved.

2.0 Criteria for Approval of District Programs

In approving district programs or interdistrict programs of in-service preparation in the history, culture, and current problems of racial and ethnic minorities, the Department of Education has the responsibility to determine that:

* the programs address the needs of teachers and other school staff in preparing to relate to minority-group students in the particular school (see Section 2.1);

* planning involves school staff, as well as adults and (where appropriate) high school students who are members of the minority groups served by participating schools (see Section 2.2);

* the programs are adequate in terms of scope, relevance and quality (see Section 2.3);

* the format and time frame meet at least minimum standards (see Section 2.4);

* instructors and resources are the best available for the purpose of these courses (see Section 2.5);

* there is a bona fide effort to promote maximum participation by the staff of participating schools (see Section 2.6);

* the programs will be evaluated and reports made to facilitate their improvement (see Section 2.7);

2.1 Identification of Participating Schools

2.1.1 The school district shall use data from the latest racial and ethnic survey to identify all the schools, primary, intermediate and secondary, in which minority-group students comprise 25 percent or more of total enrollment. The teachers and other professional staff of each such school are those for whom in-service preparation is to be provided, either by the district or by two or more cooperating districts.

2.1.2 From the survey data, the district shall identify the minority groups which are represented in substantial numbers in the student population of each participating school. In-service preparation courses and programs shall be designed primarily to address the needs of teachers and other staff to understand and relate to the history, culture, and current problems of those groups. They should also take cognizance of the history, culture, and current problems of students of other ethnic backgrounds in the district. It is expected that in-service courses will give attention to the sources of prejudice, discrimination and conflict relating to any other of the diverse groups in the public schools.

2.2 The Planning Process

In order to provide a program addressed to improving the ability of school staff to meet the needs of minority-group students, the school district or cooperating districts should convene a planning committee and enable it to meet and prepare a recommended program.

2.2.1 The planning committee should include one or more teachers, principals, parents, and other adults from the community, and, if a high school is involved, students. The planning committee should reflect the diversity of ethnic backgrounds in the district, and at least half of the committee should be representative of the minority groups enrolled in participating schools.

2.2.2 The advice of teacher organizations and of existing parent or community advisory committees should be asked and should be considered by the planning committee.

2.2.3 The planning committee should be given an explanation of the law and guidelines and should meet at least twice. In addition to making recommendations for program content and format, the committee should advise regarding resources for in-service curriculum and instruction.

2.3 Scope, Relevance and Quality of Programs

2.3.1 In-service preparation programs for this purpose consist of courses designed to relate to the themes, concepts, and issues listed in Section 1.5 above, as well as specifically to the history, culture, and current problems of those minority groups present in each school.

2.3.2 Within the district program, teachers and other professional staff may be offered various optional courses, providing each option is consistent with the requirements stated in these guidelines.

2.3.3 Each program should include practical experience applying to the education of minority-group students, such as home visits, field activities, interviews, and classroom projects.

2.3.4 Courses and programs shall be evaluated according to standards of quality commensurate with those applied to other in-service programs of the district or districts, and according to realistic objectives consistent with the goals stated in Section 1.4 above.

2.4 Format and Time Frame

2.4.1 Each program plan submitted to the Department of Education must contain a subject-matter outline for each course in sufficient detail to make possible a determination as to the scope of the program and its relevance to the requirements of Article 3.3.

2.4.2 Each teacher and other member of professional staff at a participating school should be encouraged to complete 60 to 90 hours of instruction and field activities (four to six semester units) in these in-service courses. A major portion of the in-service preparation for each person should emphasize the history, culture, and current problems of each minority group which is present in substantial numbers at that school.

2.4.3 Every district with one or more participating schools as defined in Section 2.1 above shall provide an in-service program meeting the requirements of these guidelines. Initial implementation should begin during the school year 1973-74. The program should continue during 1974-75 and 1975-76 in order to achieve the goal of maximum participation by school staff no later than June 1976.

2.4.4 Two or more school districts may cooperate in planning, submitting for approval, and conducting programs of in-service preparation. Coordination may be provided by the appropriate county departments of education.

2.5 Instructors and Resources

It is considered essential that in-service preparation courses be presented by competent instructors with participation by well-informed, articulate resource persons who are from the minority and ethnic groups present in participating schools.

2.5.1 The planning committee should have an opportunity to review the qualifications of proposed instructors and resource persons and to state its recommendations.

2.5.2 The Department of Education shall publish periodically revised lists of recommended human and material resources to assist school districts in planning these courses.

2.6 Participation and Credit

Every teacher and other professional staff member at a participating school should be encouraged to complete in-service preparation courses meeting the requirements of these guidelines no later than the end of the school year 1975-76.

2.6.1 Each person who completes a course which is part of a district program should receive a certificate of completion, and, if applicable, credit for the purpose of salary increments. In addition, he may receive degree credit for appropriate courses offered by a college or university.

2.6.2 Credit also may be given for completion of other college courses if they are on the list of courses approved by the Department of Education and fulfill the requirements stated in these guidelines.

2.6.3 The district should include in its program plan all possible incentives for participation such as released time, the credits mentioned above, reimbursement of college fees, etc.

2.7 Evaluation and Reports

The district program plan submitted for Department of Education approval shall contain a design for evaluation which will measure the results of component courses in terms of the knowledge, skills, attitudes, and performance of teachers and other professional school staff who participate.

2.7.1 Objectives used in the evaluation of courses are expected to reflect the goals enumerated in Section 1.4. They should be realistic objectives, achievable within the time and circumstances of the course.

2.7.2 As of June 30 each year, beginning in 1974, the school district shall report the results of implementation of the approved program to the Department of Education. The report shall include:

a. List of courses offered during the preceding school year, with title or brief description;

b. Number of hours of instruction; number of sessions; number of (1) teachers, (2) principals, (3) other professional school staff, and (4) others, if any, who completed each course;

c. Number of teachers and other professional school staff at each participating school who have completed (1) at least 30 hours, (2) at least 60 hours, and (3) 90 hours or more of instruction in the program;

d. Number of those who have completed less than 30 hours of instruction and those who have not completed any part of the program.

2.7.3 The district report shall include a summary of the evaluation of results of each course in terms of the knowledge, skills, attitudes, and performance of teachers and other professional school staff who participate and their reactions to the in-service course work.

2.7.4 The Department of Education shall report annually to the Legislature the plans of districts to comply with these requirements, the extent of participation, and the results of programs as evaluated.

3.0 Criteria for Approval of College Courses

In approving courses offered by community colleges and other colleges and universities, the Department of Education, in consultation with the college or the appropriate State higher education agency, has the responsibility to determine that:

* there is consultation with school districts regarding plans for the courses, so that they are appropriate for district in-service needs and include practical application of learning to school situations (see Section 3.1);

* the format and time frame meet at least minimum standards (see Section

3.2);

* college personnel are informed of human and material resources available for the purpose of these courses (see Section 3.3);

* appropriate credit is provided upon completion of each course (see Section 3.4);

* the courses will be evaluated by the school districts in terms of the knowledge, skills, attitudes, and performance of teachers and other staff who have participated (see Section 3.5).

3.1 Scope and Relevance of Courses

3.1.1 A course to be approved by the Department of Education shall be designed to relate specifically to the themes, concepts, and issues listed in Section 1.3 or to the history, culture, and current problems of a minority or ethnic group or groups.

3.1.2 Each course to the extent that is feasible, shall include not only academic instruction, but also practical experience through field-work or projects applying to the education of minority-group students.

3.2 Format and Time Frame

3.2.1 Each course proposal submitted to the Department of Education shall contain a subject-matter outline in sufficient detail to make possible a determination as to the scope of each course and its relevance to district in-service programs under these guidelines.

3.2.2 A course shall require the equivalent of at least 15 hours of instruction (one semester-unit).

3.3 Lists of Resources and of Approved Courses

The Department of Education shall publish periodically revised lists of approved courses and of recommended human and material resources related to these courses and to district programs.

3.4 Credit

Colleges shall grant graduate credit for those courses which are conducted at the graduate level and for which teachers and other school staff are properly enrolled. They shall notify school districts regarding successful completion of courses, so that the district may keep a record and the teachers and other school staff may receive salary increment or other district credits.

3.5 Reports and Evaluation

Each college course included in an approved school district program shall be evaluated by the district, according to its evaluation design, in terms of the knowledge, skills, attitudes and performance of teachers and other professional school staff who have participated. The district shall include a summary of this evaluation in its annual report to the State Department of Education.

APPENDIX D

HISPANIC URBAN CENTER

In-Service Program for Teachers and Administrators

Working with Mexican American Students

The Hispanic Urban Center offers an in-service program to teachers and administrators leading to a greater awareness, understanding, and background for creating an effective learning environment for Mexican American students.

Workshops

#100--The Mexican American in the Schools

The Mexican American in the Schools is an in-service workshop designed to provide participants with information that will lead to a greater awareness of the Mexican American youngsters' cultural and linguistic differences. The experience is implemented through workshops of eighteen to twenty teaching professionals studying, investigating, and dialoguing about various aspects of the cultural and language patterns of the Mexican American with recognized experts from local colleges, universities and community.

The workshops meet for a period of several days for a comprehensive review and study of the Mexican American. This initial period is followed by a series of four group meetings during the period of one academic semester. These intermittent meetings are compulsory. They are designed to aid the participant in analyzing, reviewing his ongoing experiences in the schools. Methods and techniques for achieving a more effective learning environment are presented during the semester.

The participants are expected to be actively involved in a series of community activities that should broaden their understanding of the barrio.

Reading and recommended bibliographies are provided by the workshop leaders.

Mini Courses

A series of "mini courses" are offered to broaden or to provide additional knowledge in specific areas for teachers K-12.

Prerequisite: The Mexican American in the Schools.

#201--The History of the Mexican American

The course deals with the evolvement of the Mexican American in the Southwest; the clash between the Anglo American and the Mexican American culture; the urbanization of the Mexican American; the Chicano.

#202--The Mexican American and the Arts

The course offers an analysis of Mexican and Mexican American art, music, drama, and their role in the contemporary social scene. Recommended for fine arts and social studies teachers.

#203--Mexican Literature in Translation

The student makes a study of the first chronicles of Mexico, the colonial period, patriotic writers of Independence, the Romantic period, and contemporary authors. Recommended for English and world literature teachers.

#204--The Mexican American and Literature

The course reviews the role of the Mexican American in literature from about 1800 to the present. It also reviews contemporary literature by Mexican American writers. Recommended for English, American literature, and social studies teachers.

#205--The Mexican American Adolescent

The nature of the problems of the Mexican American and Chicano adolescent are studied. The course also includes an analysis of peer group pressures, the home, the barrio, and causes for these students being alienated from school and society. Recommended for secondary teachers and counselors.

#206--Teaching Reading to the Bilingual Students

This course is designed to provide the participants with knowledge, methods and techniques that will facilitate the teaching of reading to the bilingual student. Recommended for all teachers K-12.

#207--Linguistic Problems of the Mexican American Students

This course will contrast the phonological, morphological, and syntactic aspects of Spanish and English. A study of the structure of the language, its dialects and usage problems will also be studied in order to emphasize the difficulties in second language learning for those whose native language is Spanish.

#208--Fieldwork in the Barrio

Field study observations of selected barrios, institutions and agencies will be conducted under supervision and preparatory instruction to thoroughly acquaint the participants with the barrio.

APPENDIX E

FIRST EVALUATIVE INSTRUMENT

		Percent of times or cases that this will occur.					
		0-20%	21-40%	41-60%	61-80%	81-100%	Don't know
1.	A Mexican American youth will find a youth-oriented recreation facility within one-half mile of his home.	1	2	3	4	5	6
2.	Guidance services are within easy reach of East Los Angeles families.	1	2	3	4	5	6
3.	Mexican American parents understand and speak English well.	1	2	3	4	5	6
4.	Mexican American parents encourage their daughters to go to college.	1	2	3	4	5	6
5.	Mexican American parents frequently read to their young children.	1	2	3	4	5	6
6.	Bitterness and alienation inhibit the school achievement of Mexican American elementary school children.	1	2	3	4	5	6
7.	Mexican Americans lose out on good job opportunities because they don't know how to look for them.	1	2	3	4	5	6
8.	Mexican American youth assume they won't get jobs even if they have a diploma, so why finish school?	1	2	3	4	5	6
9.	One drawback to a Mexican American's employability is his inability to read well.	1	2	3	4	5	6

68

	0-20%	21-40%	41-60%	61-80%	81-100%	Don't Know
10. The achievement problem for the Mexican American child lies in the conflict between his "Mexican" values and the middle class values of his Anglo teacher.	1	2	3	4	5	6
11. Mexican Americans miss getting jobs they could handle because they do not handle the English language well enough.	1	2	3	4	5	6
12. Mexican American families don't have enough money to care for the bare necessities.	1	2	3	4	5	6
13. Mexican American mothers lack the knowledge they need to provide their families with balanced nutrition.	1	2	3	4	5	6
14. Mexican Americans are timid about seeking jobs.	1	2	3	4	5	6
15. Medical and dental services are available to East Los Angeles families at prices they can afford.	1	2	3	4	5	6
16. There is a lack of understanding between Eastside residents and law enforcement officers.	1	2	3	4	5	6
17. Praise, not reprimand, should be used in dealing with the Mexican American child.	1	2	3	4	5	6
18. East Los Angeles school personnel understand and speak Spanish well.	1	2	3	4	5	6
19. Spiritual training is absent in Mexican American homes.	1	2	3	4	5	6

	0-20%	21-40%	41-60%	61-80%	81-100%	Don't know
20. Law enforcement officers assigned to East Los Angeles are trained in the unique problems of the area.	1	2	3	4	5	6
21. The Mexican American home is too small and crowded to provide a good spot for doing homework.	1	2	3	4	5	6
22. Employers are prejudiced against hiring Mexican Americans.	1	2	3	4	5	6
23. Mexican American youth drop out of school to help support the family.	1	2	3	4	5	6
24. Mexican American parents know many of the simple rules which promote good health.	1	2	3	4	5	6
25. Mexican Americans are employed by East Los Angeles law enforcement agencies.	1	2	3	4	5	6
26. Teachers in East Los Angeles do a good job of instructing Mexican American students.	1	2	3	4	5	6
27. Mexican American children do poorly in school because they are in poor health.	1	2	3	4	5	6
28. Mexican American parents are unable to make their teen-age children go to school.	1	2	3	4	5	6
29. Rural-oriented Mexican Americans suffer cultural shock as they enter U.S. urban society.	1	2	3	4	5	6

		0-20%	21-40%	41-60%	61-80%	81-100%	Don't know
30.	The achievement of Mexican American children tends to be below national grade level norms.	1	2	3	4	5	6
31.	Mexican Americans lack the skills they need to make them employable.	1	2	3	4	5	6
32.	Mexican Americans see other Americans with material possessions they can never expect to have.	1	2	3	4	5	6
33.	Mexican Americans lack the educational background they need to qualify for better employment.	1	2	3	4	5	6
34.	Mexican Americans settle for menial jobs because they lack high aspiration and self-esteem.	1	2	3	4	5	6
35.	Mexican American parents have a high level of aspiration for their own personal education.	1	2	3	4	5	6
36.	Mexican American parents have a high level of aspiration for their children's education.	1	2	3	4	5	6
37.	Mexican American parents encourage their sons to go to college.	1	2	3	4	5	6
38.	Mexican American families are too large for their meager family income.	1	2	3	4	5	6
39.	There is an absence of educational tradition in Mexican families coming from rural Mexico.	1	2	3	4	5	6
40.	Mexican American parents take their children to the public library.	1	2	3	4	5	6

		0- 20%	21- 40%	41- 60%	61- 80%	81- 100%	Don't know
41.	Mexican American parents come to school to find out about their children's progress.	1	2	3	4	5	6
42.	Mexican American parents lack sufficient educational background to help their children with school work.	1	2	3	4	5	6
43.	East Los Angeles school personnel have the skills they need to deal adequately with the Mexican American child.	1	2	3	4	5	6
44.	The curriculum for the Mexican American child is relevant to his personal life and background.	1	2	3	4	5	6
45.	Mexican Americans could get better employment if it were not for stereotypes that employers have about Latins, i.e., lazy, do just enough to subsist, etc.	1	2	3	4	5	6
46.	Mexican American parents provide an adequate study environment at home.	1	2	3	4	5	6
47.	Mexican Americans who have been rural-oriented don't know how to compete in the "dog eat dog" U.S. economic system.	1	2	3	4	5	6
48.	East Los Angeles teachers think that Mexican American children are good learners.	1	2	3	4	5	6
49.	Mexican Americans cannot make themselves heard by the powers that be.	1	2	3	4	5	6
50.	Mexican American children do not understand nor speak English well.	1	2	3	4	5	6

		0-20%	21-40%	41-60%	61-80%	81-100%	Don't know
51.	Mexican American teen-agers drop out of school.	1	2	3	4	5	6
52.	Mexican American children aren't with it when it comes to minding teacher, learning the times tables, and going to college.	1	2	3	4	5	6
53.	Mexican Americans don't get out of the barrio to the beaches and mountains because they can't afford it.	1	2	3	4	5	6
54.	Mexican American families are underhoused.	1	2	3	4	5	6
55.	Mexican American parents see little value in education.	1	2	3	4	5	6
56.	Mexican American parents are careless about their children's attendance and/or promptness in arriving at school.	1	2	3	4	5	6
57.	Mexican American children do not have the skills prerequisite to successful learning when they enter kindergarten and first grade.	1	2	3	4	5	6
58.	Mexican American children lose interest in school because there isn't enough there for them to identify with.	1	2	3	4	5	6
59.	Mexican American children live in a broken home.	1	2	3	4	5	6
60.	The schools demand less of the Mexican American child than he is actually capable of producing.	1	2	3	4	5	6
61.	Hospitals are easily accessible to residents of East Los Angeles.	1	2	3	4	5	6

	0-20%	21-40%	41-60%	61-80%	81-100%	Don't know
62. The schools fail to inspire and encourage the Mexican American child to shoot for goals equal to his abilities.	1	2	3	4	5	6
63. Counseling for Mexican Americans at the high school level is inadequate.	1	2	3	4	5	6
64. Mexican American parents exercise strong supervision over their children.	1	2	3	4	5	6

EDUCATION PROBLEMS

In this section, items can be subdivided by whether beliefs relate to factors in the school, factors in the learner, or factors in the home.

A. School Related

1. Services

One item (63) relates to school services. The item reads, "Counseling for Mexican Americans at the high school level is inadequate." This item drew the most "don't know" responses of any item on the pre-test. This seems to reflect the elementary school orientation of the respondents. Many probably do not know what occurs in East Los Angeles high schools. The modal value for this item on both the pre-test and the post-test was 81-100 percent. In other words, for those who think they know the situation, the tendency is to believe that counseling at the high school level is inadequate for most Mexican American students. It should be noted that there was a substantial shift away from the "don't know" category on the post-test. The belief that counseling is inadequate for most Chicano students is shared by more people after instruction than before.

2. Curriculum

Two items (44, 58) dealt with curriculum. The first of these reads, "The curriculum for the Mexican American child is relevant to his personal life and background." The modal value on both the pre-test and post-test was 0-20 percent. Teachers believe that the curriculum is relevant for relatively few Mexican American students. It would be interesting to find out what they think should be done to make the curriculum relevant.

The other item related to curriculum states, "Mexican American children lose interest in school because there isn't enough for them to identify with." Responses to this item showed no clearcut consensus. Response category selections ranged rather evenly over all possible values. Considering the shape of the total curve, the mode 61-80 percent is relatively meaningless. This is a strange result when it is considered in the light of results for item 44. On the one hand, the teachers are nearly unanimous in agreeing the curriculum is irrelevant for the Mexican American child. But they do not concur in believing that the lack of relevance (material with which to identify) is not a significant cause of the children's disinterest. It may be that the fault is ambiguity in item 58.

3. Teachers

Eight items (10, 17, 18, 26, 43, 48, 60, and 62) deal with the teacher factor. Two of these deal with teacher skill in instructing Mexican American students. Item 18 states, "East Los Angeles school personnel understand and speak Spanish well." Teachers overwhelmingly selected the 0-20 percent category both pre and post. Item 43 states, "East Los

75

Angeles school personnel have the skills they need to deal adequately with the Mexican American child." The modal value on the pre-test was 21-40 percent. In the post-test, the modal value moved to 0-20 percent. In both items, the respondents judged that there were relatively few teachers with the necessary skills. The instructional program seems to have convinced some respondents that the teacher skills deficit is more serious than they had originally judged.

When it comes to evaluating the kind of teaching turned in by East Los Angeles teachers, the respondents tend to rate them more highly than might be expected considering their own admission that they lack the requisite skills for doing the job. This conclusion follows from results for item 26: "Teachers in East Los Angeles do a good job of instructing Mexican American students." The modal value on both the pre-test and post-test was 41-60 percent. In both cases, the curve tails off evenly to each extreme. The course of instruction seems to have resulted in increased variability and lesser kurtosis. Respondents believe that teachers do a good job with at least half of their Mexican American students. This implies conversely that respondents believe that there is a substantial number of students who are not receiving good instruction.

A similar pattern of response holds for item 48: "East Los Angeles teachers think that Mexican American children are good learners." Both pre and post--the modal value is 41-60 percent. The left tail has a substantially higher frequency than the right. This seems to mean that the respondents believe that half or less of the teaching force in East Los Angeles thinks of Mexican American children as good learners. This is significant in the light of recent evidence regarding the detrimental effect of low teacher expectations on pupil performance.

Additionally, it should be noted that on the post-test, a number of respondents deserted the "don't know" category and marked responses in the quantative categories. There is a corresponding increase in the number of persons estimating the incidence of the problem in the 61-80 percent and 81-100 percent categories. Response patterns on items 60 and 62 were interesting. Item 60 reads: "The schools demand less of the Mexican American child than he is actually capable of producing." Item 62 reads: "The schools fail to inspire and encourage the Mexican American child to shoot for goals equal to his abilities." In both items on the pre-test the curve is so flat it would be meaningless to select a mode. Teachers are highly divided on these items. However, modes clearly appear on the post-test. There is a tendency toward greater agreement. The modal value for item 60 on the post-test is 41-60 percent. This seems to imply that in half or more of the cases, respondents believe that teachers do not make demands on students equal to their abilities. The modal value for item 62 is 21-40 percent. This seems to indicate that respondents believe that schools adequately inspire students to shoot for goals equal to their abilities in substantially more than half the cases. This appears contradictory with documented evidence about drop-out rates and college graduation rates for Mexican Americans. Assuming that intelligence is normally distributed in the Mexican American population, there is a wide discrepancy between achievement and potential for most Mexican American children. Item 10 deals with possible cultural conflict. "The achievement problem for the Mexican American child lies in the conflict between

his 'Mexican' values and the middle class values of his Anglo teacher."
In both the pre-test and the post-test the modal value was 41-60 percent.
Respondents apparently feel that such a conflict occurs in a substantial
number of cases and that it does tend to inhibit achievement in the child.
Since this is widely believed both by large numbers of Mexican Americans
as well as teachers, it would be useful to further explore the nature of
the conflict and precisely how it affects achievement.

The last item dealing with the teacher factor is number 17: "Praise, not
reprimand, should be used in dealing with the Mexican American child."
Response was predictable. The modal value was 81-100 percent. Practically
the whole distribution was concentrated at the upper end of the scale.

Summarizing the data related to teacher factors, we find that respondents
tend to agree that teachers in East Los Angeles lack some of the skills
requisite for dealing with Mexican American children. They believe that
in a substantial number of cases, there is a cultural conflict between
Mexican American students and their Anglo teachers and that this conflict
results in lowered achievement. They believe that a substantial number of
teachers do not think of Mexican American children as good learners. It
follows that they also believe that in a substantial number of cases
teachers do not do a good job of instructing Mexican American students.

In one area the respondents do not agree with one another. They do not
agree about whether the schools demand or inspire the children to produce
as much as they are capable of producing. Additionally it may be noted
that there were some changes between the pre-test and the post-test which
may be attributed to the instructional program. There was a growing tendency to see counseling for the Mexican American student at the secondary
level as being inadequate. There was a growing recognition of the deficiency in a special teacher skills which are requisite for teaching Chicano
children.

B. Learner Related Problems

Several items in the inventory relate to the learner. Some items deal with
symptoms: low average achievement and drop-out. Other items deal with
presumed causes: health, bitterness and alienation, language, self-
discipline, and entry skills.

1. Symptoms

    a. Drop-out

        Dropping out is a clear symptom of an educational malady. Two items
        (8, 23) ask the respondents to speculate about the reasons for
        dropping out. One states: "Mexican American youth assume they
        won't get jobs even if they have a diploma so, why finish school?"
        The mode is 21-40 percent. The other item states: "Mexican
        American youth drop out of school to help support their families."
        The distribution on the pre-test was trimodal centering equally on
        items 21-40 percent, 41-60 percent, and 61-80 percent. On the post-
        test opinion tended to shift to lower estimates with the mode at 41-

60 percent. Respondents seem to feel that both job expectations and family financial status are significant factors in drop-out cases. One item (51) asks the respondents to estimate the size of the drop-out rate: "Mexican American teen-agers drop out of school." The modal value on both tests was 41-60 percent. The distributions tend to be clustered closely around this value.

b. Achievement

Item 30 states: "The achievement of Mexican American children tends to be below national grade level norms." On both the pre-test and post-test the modal value is 81-100 percent. The curve is negatively skewed. Teachers are in agreement that the low level of achievement is widely spread throughout the population of the Mexican American children. The drop in the kurtosis on the post-test indicates a drop from the pre-test in the amount of agreement about just how widespread the problem is.

2. Causes

Several items deal with factors in the child which may pre-dispose him to poor achievement.

a. Alienation

Item 6 states: "Bitterness and alienation inhibit the school achievement of Mexican American elementary school children." The modal value on both tests was 0-20 percent. However, after the instructional program, respondents tended to see this as occurring with greater frequency than they had originally estimated.

b. Health

A second item (27) reads: "Mexican American children do poorly in school because they are in poor health." The mode was centered on 21-40 percent for the pre-test and 0-20 percent for the post-test. There was a systematic tendency for the respondents after instruction to see this problem occur with less frequency.

c. Entry Skills

Another item (57) states: "Mexican American children do not have the skills prerequisite to learning when they enter kindergarten and first grade." On the pre-test the mode was centered on 61-80 percent. On the post-test it was on 21-40 percent. While recognized as a serious problem both times, it was seen as less serious after the respondents had received the instructional program.

d. Language

Language is often mentioned as a factor in achievement. One item (50) states: "Mexican American children do not speak nor understand English well." On both the pre-test and the post-test the mode was centered on 21-40 percent. Inspection of the frequency curve shows that following instruction this problem was seen as having a slightly higher frequency than before.

e. Self-Discipline

Another item (52) says: "Mexican American children aren't with it when it comes to minding the teacher, learning the times tables, and going to college." The mode on the pre-test fell at 0-20 percent. On the post-test it fell at 21-40 percent. In spite of the perjorative nature of the item, respondents were willing to say that this holds in a substantial number of cases.

Summarizing data related to factors in the learner, the respondents demonstrate keen awareness of the dimension of the drop-out and achievement problems. They do not believe that bitterness and alienation do much to influence the achievement of younger children. Poor health is seen as having bad effects in a relatively small number of cases. A stronger contributing factor in poor achievement is lack of requisite English language skills. Respondents believe that a very large proportion of Mexican American children enter school without the prerequisite entry skills.

The following changes between pre-test and post-test may be a result of the instructional program. There was a growing tendency to see the young Mexican American child as struggling with the problem of alienation and bitterness. Estimates of the frequency with which poor health inhibits achievement were revised downward. There was a tendency to see more children entering kindergarten and first grade with skills prerequisite to successful mastery of school learning tasks. Finally, estimates of the frequency with which English language problems interfere with school achievement were revised downward.

C. Home Related Problems

1. Educational Status of Parents

Educators in East Los Angeles believe that part of the Mexican American's problems at school relate to his home background.

a. Preparation

One of the critical factors is the educational status of the parents. One item (39) states: "There is an absence of educational tradition in Mexican families coming from rural Mexico." On the pre-test the mode was 81-100 percent. On the post-test it shifted to 0-21 percent, exactly at opposite ends of the scale. This points to a substantial shift after instruction in the direction of greater respect for the kind of educational tradition which the child brings to school with him. Item 42 deals with the ability of Mexican American parents to help their children with school work: "Mexican American parents lack sufficient educational background to help their children with school work." The modal value on the pre-test was 21-40 percent. Most of the distribution stretched above that point. Thus, 90 percent of the respondents believed that 20 percent or more of parents are unable to help. On the post-test there was a substantial shift toward 0-20 percent. While the mode remained the same, the general shape of the curve changed. Following instruction, several people indicated a growing confidence in parents' competency in helping with their children's education. Most respondents, however, persist in believing that a very high proportion of parents are unable to help.

b. Attitudes

Though respondents tend to believe that parents' educational background is meager, they think that parents value education. Item 55 reads: "Mexican American parents see little value in education." The mode fell at 0-20 percent for both pre-test and post-test. The distribution tails off rapidly from there. Two items (35 and 36) deal with level of aspiration. Item 35 states: "Mexican American parents have a high level of aspiration for their own personal education." The mode for the pre-test fell at 0-20 percent and for the post-test at 21-40 percent. This modest change is consistent with other evidence to support the hypothesis that the course of instruction moved some of the learners toward a higher view of the Mexican parent as a person who values education and who can make positive contributions to the child's education. On the other hand, it should be noted that the overall shape of the distribution indicates that respondents believe that relatively few parents have high aspirations for their own education.

The picture is different when it comes to parents' level of aspiration for their children's education. Item 36 says: "Mexican American parents have a high level of aspiration for their children's education." The mode for both pre-test and post-test fell at 41-60 percent. Thus, respondents believe that a very substantial portion of parents do have such aspirations. Furthermore, the shape of the curve shows that following instruction several respondents revised their estimates of such parents upward, again indicating a small but favorable shift perhaps as a result of the instructional program.

2. Study Environment

Item 46 deals with study environment at home. It reads: "Mexican American parents provide an adequate study environment at home." The mode on the pre-test fell at 0-20 percent. The distribution on the post-test was bimodal, falling at 0-20 percent and 21-40 percent. Inspection of the curve shows that this is not an important change and that in general, respondents feel that it is relatively rare that children have a good study atmosphere at home. The reason for this feeling is perhaps given by Item 21 where respondents indicate their belief that the typical Mexican American home is too small to provide a good place for doing homework.

3. Parents' Moral Support of Child

The next set of items has to do with the frequency with which Mexican American parents take specific actions on behalf of their children's education (5, 40, 56, 4, 37, 28, and 41).

Item 5 deals with the frequency with which Mexican American parents read to their young offspring. Teachers believe this is atypical. The mode on the pre-test fell at 0-20 percent. Ninety-five percent of the respondents believed this happens in 40 percent or fewer of all cases. The location of the mode remained the same on the post-test but a substantial number of respondents had shifted to the 21-40 percent category, another evidence of improved respect for the overall educational role of the Mexican American family after taking the course.

Reading to children probably contributes positively to development of language skills. Taking children to the library probably does the same. Item 40 says: "Mexican American parents take their children to the public library." On both the pre-test and post-test the mode fell at 0-20 percent. This indicates that on the average, respondents think such parental behavior is relatively rare. However, as noted several times earlier, a shift in the shape of the distribution in the direction of higher estimates indicates a trend toward viewing the Mexican American family as a positive force in the education of children.

Do parents of Mexican American children come to school to find out about their children's school progress? The mode on both tests fell at 21-40 percent. Respondents believe this happens in less than 40 percent of the cases. Absence and tardiness are seen as serious problems by East Los Angeles personnel. Item 56 dealt with the degree to which parents contribute to the problem through negligence: "Mexican American parents are careless about their children's attendance at and promptness in arriving at school." The mode and general shape of the distribution remained stable from pre-test to post-test. About 60 percent of the respondents feel this holds in less than 40 percent of all cases.

What about the motivational function of families with respect to the children's attendance at college? Respondents believe this differs between boys and girls. Item 4 says: "Mexican American parents encourage their daughters to go to college." Item 37 is identical, except it deals with sons. The mode for daughters fell at 0-20 percent on both pre-test and post-test. For sons, both modes fell at 41-60 percent. Respondents believe that college education for sons is valued more highly than college education for daughters. On both items 4 and 37, there was a tendency to revise the estimates upward on the post-test. This tendency is most pronounced for item 37. This again argues for a positive effect of the Hispanic Urban Center instructional program in the direction of causing respondents to view the educational role of the Mexican American home in a more favorable light.

A final item (28) in this area deals with parental control over behavior of teen-age children with respect to school attendance. It reads: "Mexican American children are unable to make their teen-age children go to school." In both cases the mode fell at 21-40 percent, indicating that respondents feel this is true in 40 percent or less of all cases. The distribution shows that respondents felt after receiving instruction that parents were slightly more in control of the situation than they had originally believed.

We can summarize respondents' beliefs about the educational influence of the Mexican American home in a few sentences. The summary is based on average values as reflected by item modes. Thus they do not represent the views of 100 percent of the respondents.

Mexican American parents are seen as not doing some of the things which favor a child's language development. They tend not to read to them nor to take them to the library. They tend not to have the skills requisite to helping their children with homework. They tend not to have high aspirations for their own education. For all their personal educational deficiencies, they have relatively high aspirations for their children. Their aspirations are higher for their sons than for their daughters. In spite of this, they are unlikely to come to school to find out about their children's progress in school. They tend not, probably for economic reasons, to provide a good study environment at home.

Certain changes in belief occurred between the pre-test and the post-test. It may be that these changes can be attributed to the course of instruction. First, there was a growing tendency to see the Mexican-born parent as having an educational tradition. It follows that there would also be a growing tendency to see the Mexican parent as able to help in the education of his children. There was an increasing tendency to see the Mexican parent as one who value education, especially for his children.

THE MEXICAN AMERICAN IN THE SCHOOLS:

AN IN-SERVICE PROGRAM

A. Purpose: To meet the needs of administrators and teachers of Mexican American students by:

 1. Providing sociological-cultural information that will lead to an understanding of cultural differences between the Mexican American and the dominant society.

 2. Providing knowledge of the linguistic interferences that may occur when learning English skills.

 3. Gaining information about Mexican culture that may contribute to the cultural differences between the Mexican American and the dominant society.

 4. Studying some methods and techniques for achieving a more effective learning environment for the Mexican American student.

 5. Investigating aspects of the community that will lead to a greater comprehension and awareness of the Mexican American community.

 6. Understanding the differences among various groups within the Mexican American community.

 7. Acquiring knowledge about the Mexican and Mexican American histories and heritages that should lead to the development of more meaningful curriculum and possibly more effective methods and techniques of teaching.

 8. Analyzing problems and issues that directly affect the student in the classroom.

B. Method: The method of study will be as follows:

 1. Presentation by resource persons.

 2. Group discussions.

 3. Field trips.

 4. Individual and group reading of recommended references.

 5. Analysis of reports and statistics.

 6. Presentation of films, film strips, sound tapes, and video tapes.

 7. Individual student reports.

 8. Evaluations (self-evaluations).

<u>Texts</u>

Acuna, Rudy. <u>Occupied America.</u> Canfield Press, San Francisco: 1972.

Carter, Thomas P. <u>Mexican American in School: A History of Educational Neglect</u>. College Entrance Examination Board, New York: 1970.

McWilliams, Carey. <u>North from Mexico: The Spanish Speaking People of the United States.</u> Greenwood Press, New York: 1968.

Reading assignments from texts are noted at the top of each section in the following pages.

Unit 1: The Mexican American: Who Is He?

I. Identity of the Mexican American

Readings: McWilliams, Introduction; pp. 7-11

a. Definition of terms

b. Dynamics of change

1. Assimilation vs acculturation

2. The name game

c. Heterogeneous nature of group

1. Urban vs rural

2. Regional difference

3. The Mexican national

4. The "illegals"

d. Stereotypes

1. Origin and causes

2. Perpetuation of the myths

II. The Mexican American and the Family

a. The Continuum

b. Family roles

1. Mother

2. Father

3. Siblings

(a) Male roles

(b) Female roles

c. Extended family structure

d. Child rearing practices

e. Cultural Institutions as they relate to the family

    1. Church

    2. Community centers

    3. Social organizations

III. The Barrio

  a. Geographical and historical development

  b. Environment of the barrio

  c. Barrio vs the dominant community

  d. Economic levels

  e. Vocational opportunities

  f. Community agencies

  g. Political awareness and changes

IV. The Chicano Child: Crisis and Conflict

  a. Areas of conflict

    1. Child - family

    2. Child - school

    3. Child - larger society

  b. Gangs

    1. Membership

    2. Activities

  c. Identity Crisis

    1. Peer group pressure

    2. Graffiti

    3. Use of drugs

V. Language and Language Differences

Readings: Carter, pp. 51-53; McWilliams, pp. 290-296

  a. Language of the barrio, i.e., Calo, spanglish, tex mex, etc.

Unit 11: The History of the Mexican American
or the Making of a Minority

I. The history of the Southwest (1500-1846)

Readings: Acuna, Introduction, pp. 7-19; McWilliams, pp. 19-102, 301-304

a. Introduction

b. The Spanish "entradas"

c. The early settlements

1. The fan of settlement--Texas, New Mexico, Arizona, California and other areas

d. The Indian as viewed by the Spanish, Mexican, and Anglo

e. The role of the "Indian"

f. The romanticization of the "Spanish" heritage

g. The Spanish-Mexican attempts to hold onto the Southwest

h. The Texas revolution

II. The History of the Southwest (1846-1900)

Readings: Acuna, pp. 19-31, 34-52, 55-118; McWilliams, pp. 102-162

a. The Mexican-American War

1. The causes

2. The war

3. The aftermath

b. The role of the "Indian" during this period

c. "Open warfare" (1860-1880)

1. Filibustering expeditions

2. Black insurrection

3. Cart War

4. Cortina War

5. Salt War

III. Immigration (1900-1970)

Readings: Acuna, pp. 123-150, 190-195; McWilliams, pp. 259-274

a. The pattern of immigration

b. Waves of immigration, 1900-1910, 1910-1930

c. Restrictionist - Nativism

d. Depression - Repatriation

e. 1950s

f. Bracero Program (1942-1964)

g. The Dixon-Arnett Bill: Its Implications

IV. Labor in the Southwest

Readings: Acuna, pp. 153-218; McWilliams, pp. 162-199, 206-226.

a. Economic development

   1. Agricultural industries

      (a) Sugar beets

      (b) Citrus

      (c) Cotton

      (d) Truck farming

   2. Early transportation and railroads

   3. Mining

      (a) Gold

      (b) Silver

      (c) Copper

   4. Cattle and sheep

b. Labor supply

   1. Coyote

   2. The labor contractor (enganchistra)

c. Use of Mexican labor

   1. Availability

2. Adaptability

3. Existence of "buffer" group

4. Effect of mechanization

5. Pattern of employment

    (a) Characteristics

    (b) "Colonias"

    (c) Role of trade unions

d. Mexican labor organizations

1. The myth of docility (1920s)

2. Labor organization in the copper mines

3. Strike activity in the 20s and 30s

4. (CUOM) Confederacion de Uniones Oberaras Mexicanas (1927)

5. The Gallup Incident (1930s)

Unit 111: The Mexican American in Today's Society or the Chicano Generation

I. The Community and the School

Readings: Acuna, pp. 227-231, 235, 236, 242; Carter, pp. 14, 15, 65, 66, 67-70, 74-76, 81-86, 99-106, 109-114

a. Historical role of community

b. Community and school conflicts

c. De facto-De jure Segregation

d. School goals and the community

1. Administrators

2. Teachers

3. Teacher-aides

4. Other staff

II. The Chicano Generation

a. Composition

b. Philosophy and Ideaology

c. Chicano Creative Arts

d. Efforts

e. Successes

III. Education and the Chicano

Readings: Acuna, pp. 146, 147; Carter, pp. 3, 35, 36, 39, 47-49, 53-59, 73, 78-80, 83-86, 95-99, 116-121, 147, 160, 168, 173, 192, 203, 204, 207, 208; McWilliams, pp. 280-284, 298-301.

a. School's historical view of the Mexicano

b. Role of the school

c. Theory of cultural deprivation

d. Creation of negative self-concept

e. Chicano achievement and participation in school

f. School personnels' fears and anxieties

g. Chicanos' attitudes and perspectives

h. Teachers' attitudes and perspectives

i. Cultural exclusion

IV. Other Institutional aspects

Readings: Acuna pp. 222-227; Carter, pp. 71, 72, 77, 124-128, 170; McWilliams, pp. 226-228.

a. Government and legal systems

1. Local

2. State

3. Federal

b. Boards of Education

c. News media

d. Business and economy

e. Religion

f. Art and community activities

g. Public services

h. Professions: co-optation as an institution

Unit IV: Teaching the Mexican American
and the Chicano Student

I. Bilingual-Bicultural Education

Readings: Carter, pp. 16, 18, 49-51, 94, 114-116, 139, 153, 154, 156-168, 187-198

a. Definition

b. Cultural pluralism

c. Programs

d. Testing

e. Spanish as a second language (SSL)

f. English as a second language (ESL)

g. Language as a key to learning

II. Teacher Expectations and Implications

Readings: Carter, pp. 18, 20, 59, 87-91, 134-136, 158, 160, 174, 175

a. Learning theory

1. Teacher-learner interaction

2. Frustration level - anxiety level

3. Environment

4. Relevancy

b. Effective use of teacher aides

c. The parent's role in instruction

1. As a resource

2. As a community liasion

d. The arts and "culture" of the Mexican, Mexican American, Spanish, Indian, etc.

    1. Rationale

    2. Effective use of teacher aides

    3. The parent's role in instruction

III. Chicano-Anglo Group Patterns and Psychodynamics

    Readings: Carter, pp. 138-140, 142, 184

    a. Personal interaction

    b. Group interaction

    c. Subjective states of mind

    d. Human needs, fears, etc.

    e. Concepts of coloration

    f. Manipulation vs actualization

IV. Contemporary issues and the Mexican American Student

    Readings: Carter, pp. 87-93, 106-108, 149-153, 169, 170, 172, 173, 175-180, 185, 186, 205, 206, 210, 211, 214, 215, 217-221

    a. Education

        1. Trends

        2. Changes

            (a) Curriculum

            (b) School structure

            (c) Integration vs desegregation

            (d) Teacher preparation

    b. Community

        1. Involvement

            (a) Parent-advisory groups

            (b) Parent-teacher-student associations

        2. Opportunities

c. Government

    1. Programs

    2. Political pressures

    3. Legislation

Areas of Emphasis

I. Identify the Mexican American

a. Define the various labels used by "Mexican Americans" to identify them-selves, e.g., Mexican, Mejicano, Hispano, Latino, Mexican American, Mexican-American, Spanish American, Indio-Hispano, Chicano, etc.

b. Discuss how you identify a Mexican American in the classroom.

c. Illustrate the differences between assimilation and acculturation. Which of the two is implemented in the schools? Why?

d. Question the concept of the "name game." What causes it to exist?

e. Explain the Chicano Movement in terms of the community, the family and the schools. What are its positive aspects; its negative aspects?

f. Compare the urban Mexican American with the dominant society. Compare the Mexican American with the rural Mexican American.

g. Describe the differences that exist between Mexican Nationals and Mexican Americans. What are some of the appelations used in the barrio to iden-tify the national? What problems does the national face in the "schools"?

h. Seek out and discuss some of the stereotypic characteristics attributed to the Mexican as found in literature (see Cecil Robinson's With the Ears of Strangers, writings of John Steinbeck and other popular American authors.)

i. List and compare stereotypes of the Anglo and the Mexican, e.g., social structure, ethics, etc.

j. Explain such expressions as: "manana land, . . . but you don't look Mexican, sleepy Mexican town, cisco, machismo, happy brown faces in the sun, etc."

k. Review how various types of communication have contributed to the perpetu-ation of the stereotype. Review how the classroom teacher contributes to the perpetuation of the myths.

l. Compare the Mexican with other minorities--Black and the Mexican, Japanese and the Mexican, Jew and the Mexican.

II. The Mexican American and the Family

    a. Explain the continuum of <u>Mejicano</u> to Anglo. What are some of the cultural differences that might exist between the two ends of the continuum in terms of family structure, language, attitudes toward some of the issues or problems that exist in the community?

    b. React to how the Chicano sees the continuum as working. Discuss the difference between the melting pot theory and the separateness that many Chicanos may advocate.

    c. Discuss some of the overlaps that tend to exist between the rural Mexican and the urban Mexican in such areas as health, respect and obedience, sex roles, etc.

    d. Describe in general terms the roles of various members of a Mexican American family as they play them in every day living. Compare them to an Anglo American family. What implications may be drawn from the comparison?

    e. Describe in broad general terms what an average Mexican American family might be like in terms of daily living experiences. Do the same for a Mexican family, a newly arrived family from a rural area (legal and illegal).

    f. List some of the typical child rearing practices of an average middle class Anglo American family. Point out where differences might exist between them and those of an average Mexican American middle class family, a low socio-economic family, a Mejicano family.

    g. Discuss the role of the Catholic Church in the life of Mexican Americans. Other religious groups.

    h. List various community agencies or centers that play a role in the lives of the people of that community. Estimate and explain their successes and failures in terms of effecting a change.

III. The <u>Barrio</u>

    a. Define <u>barrio</u>. How does it differ from a community or a neighborhood?

    b. Describe the <u>barrio</u> of the community in which you are working. What is its extent, population, socio-economic level? How does it generally compare to the overall community?

    c. List the various industries or enterprises that support the community. What places do the citizens of the <u>barrio</u> hold in these economic endeavors?

    d. Report on the history of the <u>barrio</u> in your community. How does it compare with the origin of other <u>barrios</u>?

    e. List the various agencies, governmental and social, that function in the community. What are their objectives? Which are meeting those objectives?

    f. Research the development of political groups in the Mexican American community which are the most influential groups at present and what have been the issues they have supported or fought?

    g. Give several reasons why Mexican Americans have not been successful politically. Analyze and discuss the various reasons you present. Offer corrective measures.

    h. Analyze the statistics dealing with income, employment, etc. that deal with Mexican Americans or Spanish surnamed Americans.

    i. List the various vocational opportunity agencies of the Mexican American community. What do they offer? Who sponsors them? How successful have they been?

    j. Discuss the areas of conflict that exist between the barrio and the dominant community. What solutions are being offered on a local, state, and national level?

IV. The Chicano Child: Crisis and Conflict

    a. Determine some of the differences between a Mexican American child and Anglo American child; and an adolescent. What creates the differences?

    b. Discuss some of the areas of conflict that a Mexican American youngster may have with his family. How would this be different with a youngster that identifies as a Chicano?

    c. Analyze areas of conflict between a Mexican American youngster and the school situation. Are the areas of conflict symptoms or problems? Trace the source of the problems.

    d. Summarize how a Mexican American may view the world outside of the barrio. Why does he reflect these feelings?

    e. Discuss the causes and effects of gang memberships and activities in the barrio.

    f. Discuss the identity crisis faced by young people in general. What are the various outlets for the tensions created by this crisis? Which are the ones generally used by Mexican American youngsters? What alternatives can you offer for those you consider negative in nature?

    g. Discuss some of the marked differences among Mexican American girls compared to Anglo American girls. Estimate the causes for these differences. How are these differences reflected in the classroom?

    h. Discuss some of the problems faced by the counselors and teachers in attempting to offer counsel or guidance to Mexican American children. Determine the reasons for the difficulties involved. Offer some suggestions for the elimination of the obstacles involved in communication with the youngsters, with their families, etc.

V.   Language and Language Differences

   a.   Discuss some of the reasons for language differences noted among the
        people of the Mexican American community.

   b.   Describe some of the barrio dialects.

   c.   Discuss the importance of establishing language development before
        there is reading.

   d.   Give specific examples of how language reflects culture.

   e.   Make a list of the most common language interferences that exist among
        Spanish speakers who also may speak English.

   f.   Define bilinguality. How is the degree or level of language profici-
        ency determined in a bilingual?

Unit II: The History of the Mexican American
or the Making of a Minority

I.   The History of the Southwest (1500-1846)

   a.   Establish the stage on which the history of the Mexican American de-
        veloped, i.e., the geography, the people, the cultures, etc.

   b.   Evaluate the Southwest or Aztlan as to the culture that existed before
        the arrival of Europeans and Mestizos. What were its contributions to
        the intruding cultures? What did the intruders offer it? What new
        culture did the social intercourse create?

   c.   Describe the trends or phases of development that took place between
        1500-1846.

   d.   Discuss the various perspectives involved in describing the events that
        took place before the Anglo American intrusion, i.e., how did the
        Spanish or Mexican colonists view their situation?

   e.   Interpret the Texas Revolution from two distinctly different view
        points, the Anglo American and the Mexican.

II. The History of the Southwest (1846-1900)

   a.   Interpret "Manifest Destiny." What did manifest destiny mean to those
        who were invaded?

   b.   Describe the new people created by the Treaty of Guadalupe Hidalgo.
        How does the expression "to become a minority" apply?

   c.   Discuss the Indian in terms of the various intrusions. What did the
        Spanish-Mexican intrusion contribute to the Indians' world? What did
        the Anglo American contribute?

d. List some of the attempts made by the first Mexican American to hold onto their identity. How are these attempts generally viewed by historians and writers of this period?

e. Review the characteristics of the "Mexican" stereotype. How did these relate to historical events?

III. Immigration (1900-1970)

a. Discuss the reasons or motivating forces which produced these waves.

b. How were these characteristics similar or different from other groups of immigrants?

c. Write a short description of the repatriation of Mexicans during the depression. Compare it to the events in United States history, e.g., Indian wars, Indian reservations, American Japanese, and World War II, Chinese coolies and "Chinatowns," etc.

d. Describe the Mexican American service man during World War II, Korean War, the present "war."

e. Describe how the bracero program has affected relations in the barrios. What did the program mean to the labor movements, to the farmers, to the large merchants, etc.?

f. Discuss recent legislative dealing with immigration and labor that directly affects the Mexican American communities.

IV. Labor in the Southwest

a. List the various major industries of the Southwest. Beside each listing list the origin of each industry.

b. Describe the historical development of any five industries whose origin can be attributed to a Mestizo culture.

c. Describe the development of communications and transportation in the Southwest. Determine in what way there is an indebtedness to the Mexican American for its development.

d. Discuss America's endless demands for cheap labor. How does this demand affect the various minorities of the United States?

e. Review the agricultural labor movement from 1926 to 1972.

f. Establish what the new demographic trends are as to the Mexican American. What are the implications for the classroom teachers?

g. Discuss current statistics involving the Mexican American as to labor, trades, income, age groups, birthrates. In general dialogue about those characteristics commonly used to identify him as a minority. Compare these to previous ones; draw conclusions.

h. Determine where the Mexican American stands today in terms of the changing society. What has been the effect of the various positions the Chicano community has taken in terms of labor, politics, social equality?

Unit III: The Mexican American in Today's Society
of the Chicano Generation

I.   The Community and the School

a. Trace the history of the Mexican American community in terms of education since 1965 to the present.

b. Describe the various areas of conflict existing between schools and the Chicano community. What are the demands of the Chicano community as to language, integration, textbooks, administrators, teachers, etc.? How are these demands received by the dominant community? Give various Anglo American points of view. Is the Mexican American community united in its effort? Explain.

II.   The Chicano Generation

a. Describe a Chicano. How does a Chicano differ from a Mexican American?

b. List changes in the community that are Chicano in origin. What effect have these changes had on the younger members of the barrio?

c. Give examples of the Chicano corazon, i.e., the innermost expression of the self. Why are some of these self-expressions controversial?

III.   Education and the Chicano

a. Describe educational programs prior to 1966 that provided for the Mexican American and his cultural differences.

b. Investigate the subtleties involved in creating a negative self-image. How have schools employed some of these techniques?

c. Define "culturally disadvantaged," "culturally deprived," and "culturally different." Compare the definitions.

d. Determine what has created anxieties and fears among teachers since the advent of the Civil Rights Movement.

e. Analyze tests, testing procedures, evaluations, evaluators, and so forth, that are involved in determining the potential of culturally different youngsters.

f. Study the backgrounds of an average faculty of a barrio school. Determine its strengths and weaknesses, based on its background profile, in providing a learning environment for the culturally different student. Offer solutions for those areas that tend to indicate creation of a weak learning environment.

IV. Other Institutional Aspects

    a. Describe the role played by various institutions, other than educational, in limiting the opportunities for the growth and development of Mexican Americans.

    b. Give specific examples of failure of the news media to provide fair coverage of events involving the Chicano community.

    c. Discuss the role of religious institutions in the Mexican American community. What are some of their successes, some of their failures?

    d. Determine why Mexican Americans feel that certain type of employment or professions are beyond their expectations. What evidence is there to substantiate these beliefs?

<h2 style="text-align:center">Unit IV: Teaching the Mexican American and
the Chicano Student</h2>

I. Bilingual-Bicultural Education

    a. Define cultural pluralism.

    b. Sketch out a social studies unit that would provide a lesson in cultural pluralism.

    c. Devise a sales-plan for selling bilingual-bicultural education to a community.

    d. Determine several testing techniques for determining the various language levels in an average classroom.

    e. Distinguish the difference between bilingual education and ESL.

    f. Interpret the statement: Language is the key to learning. How does this apply in a barrio school?

II. Teacher Expectations and Implications

    a. Describe some of the characteristics common to the learning style of Mexican Americans. What determines these characteristics?

    b. List methods and techniques used by teachers that tend to frustrate children in a state of language development.

    c. Suggest ways of determining what is relevant to a child.

    d. Describe what might be a proper learning environment for a culturally different child. Justify the various components.

    e. List various functions that a teacher aide can perform in the classroom. How much teacher responsibility can be delegated to an aide?

    f.   Devise a plan for effective parent participation in school programs.

    g.   Suggest methods and techniques for integrating the culture and arts of the community into the school program.

III.   Chicano-Anglo group Patterns and Psychodynamics

    a.   Determine how it is that a Mexican American student feels he is different from the majority of society.

    b.   Discuss how Mexican Americans came to gain such adjectives as: docile, uninterested, passive, non-aggressive, etc.

    c.   Describe the behavior of Mexican Americans in various types of school activities, such as general classroom, playground, hall committees, small groups, etc.

    d.   Compare various behavior patterns among Anglo American adolescents with those of Mexican Americans. Do the same for children 5-12 years of age.

    e.   Estimate the greatest areas of fear and anxiety faced by Mexican American children. How do these compare with Anglo American children? Why the difference, if there is one?

    f.   Give vignettes or incidents that you feel are typical Mexican American or Chicano behavior patterns. Why do you feel these behavior patterns are typical from Anglo American youngsters?

    g.   Discuss various control methods that tend to be effective with Mexican youngsters, Anglo American youngsters, Black youngsters.

IV.   Contemporary Issues and the Mexican American Student

    a.   Describe the new trends in the education of barrio children. How many of them are spontaneous, that is to say, originating from the school? Which are the result of community pressure or federal grant or legislation?

    b.   Estimate the success of such programs, e.g., bilingual-bicultural education, ESL and SSL, reading task forces, ESEA, Title 1, integration (Title IV) community participation.

    c.   Discuss community attitudes as to integration and disegregation. How are they tangential to Black or Oriental attitudes?

    d.   Evaluate teacher preparation programs you have experienced. Give pros and cons for each.

    e.   If parent advisory groups are assumed to be a success, give reasons for that success. If they are the opposite, give the reasons.

f. Review the various legislative acts that have directly affected the education of minority groups. Give the objectives for the program you list.

g. List areas where legislation is needed in order to improve the education of Mexican American and Chicanos. Determine the role pressure groups could play in supporting such programs. How could teachers stimulate action? How should teachers' professional organizations aid in such endeavors?

APPENDIX H

MEXICAN AMERICANS IN THE SOUTHWEST:

A SURVEY OF CURRENT PERCEPTIONS

Humans have a marvelous capacity for growth and change. Where one's "head is at" at a given point in time does not, therefore, type him. You are a person in process. Even so, it would be helpful to us to get the current status of your perceptions with respect to the following 40 statements. You can indicate this by responding to the statements using the system shown below:

                5 - strongly agree
                4 - agree - yes
                3 - neither agree nor disagree - no opinion
                2 - disagree - no
                1 - strongly disagree

For example, if you very strongly agree with the first statement, then you should place a 5 on the line in front of this statement. If you strongly disagree with the statement, you place a 1 on the line. Use codes 2, 3, and 4 in a similar way. Please respond to each item.

_____ 1. The terms "Spanish American" and "Mexican American" validly distinguish between two groups with different cultural and racial origins.

_____ 2. The best way to characterize the relationship between Mexican American and Anglo in the U. S. is that of conquered and conqueror, respectively.

_____ 3. Politically and economically speaking, Mexican Americans are better off now than they would have been if the Southwest had remained a part of Mexico.

_____ 4. Most disruptive tactics used by Mexican Americans have been in support of legitimate grievances and used only after it was clear that other channels were unresponsive.

_____ 5. Mexican American parents value education, but reject the school as an educational institution.

_____ 6. There is a strong positive relation between a Mexican American child's achievement in school and the openness of community opportunity for political, economic, and cultural self-determination.

_____ 7. Mexican Americans in the Southwest are primarily an agricultural people.

_____ 8. Anglos found Mexicans in the Southwest a free, resourceful, self-governing people and quickly converted them into a landless, possessionless, politically managed, culturally maligned and physically abused people.

_____ 9. If exploitation means taking the goods and services of a people without just remuneration, then U. S. citizens of Mexican origin have been an exploited people.

_____ 10. Mexicans in the U. S. have been prized chiefly because of their capacity to do hard, dirty work for low wages.

_____ 11. Mexicans have gladly emigrated to the U. S. for a chance to improve their economic lifestyle.

_____ 12. The only effective power currently in the hands of Mexican Americans is the power to disrupt.

_____ 13. If "school adjustment" does not parallel "child adjustment," little can be done to help the Mexican American child reach his potential.

_____ 14. Law enforcement officers, assigned to barrio areas are typically trained in the unique problems of the area.

_____ 15. Experience has shown that the majority of Mexicans tend to be artistic and musical.

_____ 16. Frequently, Mexican Americans could get better jobs if it weren't for unfavorable stereotypes that employers have about Latins, i.e., lazy, do just enough to subsist, etc.

_____ 17. The academic failure of many Mexican American children is due largely to the joint failure of the child's home and culture.

_____ 18. The position of Chicanos in 1973 with respect to the judicial system remains as it was in 1850: they are seldom judged by their peers because their peers are seldom chosen for jury duty.

_____ 19. Manipulation of Mexico's economy by U. S. business has contributed to the economic subjugation of the Mexican American in the United States.

_____ 20. Most Mexican Americans settle for menial jobs because they lack high aspiration and self-esteem.

_____ 21. Most schools fail to inspire and encourage the Mexican American child to shoot for goals that equal his abilities.

_____ 22. It is unfair to let any child grow up monolingual in an area where two languages are spoken.

_____ 23. One factor that inhibits the academic performance of the Mexican American child is the fact that he lives in barrios which fail to provide equal opportunity for political, economic, and cultural self-determination.

_____ 24. The integration of Mexican Americans into U. S. society should follow the pattern provided by the Irish, Italians, Germans, and other immigrant groups.

_____ 25. With few exceptions, Mexican Americans have enjoyed equal protection of the law.

26. Bilingualism is a primary cause of the poor academic performance of the average Mexican American student.

27. A majority of teachers of Mexican American students believe that United States culture is superior to Mexican culture.

28. In most cities of the Southwest, Mexican American children have equal educational opportunity with the children of other groups.

29. The present day Southwest can be seen as Mexican territory seized through planned U. S. aggression with avarice the leading motive.

30. U. S. citizens of Mexican origin are currently denied the rights of political self-determination.

31. Anglos have not had confidence in Mexican Americans as a group to participate intelligently in democratic government.

32. Big labor has shown its commitment to upgrading the social and economic status of all workers through its support of Mexicans and other minorities in labor organizing activities.

33. Law enforcement in the Southwest has frequently been used to support and extend Anglo privilege.

34. As they relate to Mexicans, Anglos must confess that they, like all conquering peoples, have fallen prey to behaviors which reflect the "we beat them in war, so we must be superior" syndrome.

35. A partial solution to educational problems in the Southwest borderlands is a commitment to bilingual/bicultural education for both Anglos and Mexicans.

36. One cause of tension between barrio residents and law enforcement personnel is the latter's relative disregard of Mexican Americans' constitutional rights.

37. The curriculum as taught for the Mexican American child in the Southwest is relevant to his personal life and background.

38. Mexican American parents have a high level of aspiration for their children's education.

39. A Chicano arrested for a given crime has a higher probability of being roughed-up by the police than an Anglo arrested for the same crime.

40. The bitterness and alienation of many Mexican American elementary school children inhibit their school achievement.

APPENDIX I

HISPANIC URBAN CENTER

Program of In-service Education Evaluation Report

School Year 1972-1973

Introduction

The typical Mexican American child is far below the national norms in all areas of academic achievement. This problem, although it has existed for decades, has only recently become a matter of public concern. It is a concern to school districts because it represents a failure of districts to fulfill their own declared mission to provide equal educational opportunity. But most notably, it is a matter of concern to the Mexican American community because it involves the issue of personal fulfillment for the community's children. The problem is complex and its solution will require the immediate cooperation and good faith of school districts, the Mexican American community and all segments of society.

No good can come from groups blaming one another for creating this problem. The time is past when school districts can take refuge in the assumption that the roots of the problem lie in some presumed deficiencies in the children's culture. The time is also past when the community can lay all blame on school districts. Everyone, therefore, must start with the basic assumption that behavior has multiple causes and that nothing short of a many-pronged attack aimed at elimination of the causes will suffice.

A start has been made through Los Angeles community efforts to improve the relevance of textbook adoptions, and by the school district to improve reading through criterion referenced instruction. The use of community aides in classroom activities also has been helpful.

But what other areas of possible action remain? There has long been a feeling that the classroom teacher is one critical variable in any child's education. Lewin, Lippitt, and White (1939) showed that authoritarian versus democratic teacher leadership have predictable results in children's behavior. Other studies using varieties of techniques for studying teacher-student interaction have demonstrated similar effects (Remmers, 1963). Most recently Rosenthal and Jacobson (1968) have demonstrated that teacher expectations affect student achievement. Though the latter study suffered numerous methodological defects, there is little doubt about the reality of the phenomenon it attempted to demonstrate.

If the teacher is always central to what happens in learning, can it be that the teacher is central to the problem in East Los Angeles, and if so, in what sense? The research cited above definitely implicates the teacher but not in any malicious sense. Any reasonable approach to the teacher must assume that he or she is an ally, not an enemy. There is no reason to believe that teachers in East Los Angeles are anything but intelligent persons who are pursuing professional goals in good faith and acting in a way which they assume to be in the best interests of their students.

Is it possible then that teachers whose intent is to act in their students' best interest unwittingly act otherwise? The Rosenthal study seems to indicate that such things do happen. The staff of the Hispanic Urban Center takes this as a foundational assumption underlying the work described in this paper.

The Hispanic Urban Center Program

The program was a course of study, 15 weeks in length, 3 hours per week. The course was designed by Professor Luis Felipe Hernandez and revised by Mr. Tony Ortiz. The course deals with four areas of content: (1) the identity of the Mexican American child with emphasis on the family, the community, the culture, and the language; (2) the history of the Mexican American; (3) the Mexican American in today's society, focusing on his political and economic experience; and (4) ways to improve the education of the Mexican American child.

The course was offered in the Fall of 1972 and again in the Spring of 1973. The course content was delivered through a variety of learning activities. These included lectures by course instructors and visiting resource persons, and group discussions, field trips, audio-visual presentations, writing and reading. Reading included a basic core of text books plus especially selected articles. The text books used were: Occupied America (Rudolfo Acuna); The Mexican American in the Schools: A History of Educational Neglect (Thomas Carter); and North from Mexico (Carey McWilliams). The course earns a graduate credit from Occidental College.

Participant and Comparison Groups

The persons participating in both sessions were all members of faculties of elementary schools in Title 1 and Model Cities areas of the Los Angeles City Unified School District. Only faculties of schools with a majority of Spanish surnamed students were invited. Enrollment was voluntary. Some schools had close to 100% faculty enrollment. Others had much less. The degree to which administrators applied subtle pressure in favor of enrollment is not known.

The comparison group was formed by matching schools in the Fall participant group with non-participating schools on the basis of four principal criteria: (1) proportion of Spanish surnamed students, (2) school size, (3) location, and (4) participation in the Title 1 Program. The results of the matching can be observed in Tables 4 and 5. There it may be observed that proportions between groups within categories are very similar. The participant groups tended to be somewhat younger, less experienced, and more heavily loaded with persons who identify themselves as members of clearly identifiable minority groups.

The Chicano Awareness Scale

The Chicano Awareness Scale, was modeled after the Dogmatism Scale (Rokeach, 1960) and the Inventory of Beliefs (Stern, Stein, and Bloom, 1956). The theory behind items in this scale is that people possess beliefs that vary along the dimension of centrality. A belief that is truly central is one which, if it is changed, results in changes in beliefs, life style, expressed likes and dislikes, friendships, etc. (Rokeach, 1968).

To what degree do an Anglo American's beliefs about Mexican Americans affect his interaction with them? The presumption is that to the degree that beliefs are central, the effects are momentous. Is it possible for an Anglo American to hold